FIELD SPORTS LIBRARY

A HUNTING PAGEANT

OTHER BOOKS AVAILABLE

Famous Foxhunters
Daphne Moore

The Waterloo Cup
H. Edwardes Clarke

Great Horses of Britain
Lee Weatherley

Animals of the Countryside
Guy N. Smith

Hounds in Old Days
Sir Walter Gilbey, Bart

Hounds of France
George Johnston and Maria Ericson

The Concise History of the Shire Horse
Sir Walter Gilbey, Bart

A HUNTING PAGEANT

by

Mary S. Lovell

Mary S Lovell

Published by:

SAIGA PUBLISHING CO. LTD.
1 Royal Parade, Hindhead, Surrey GU26 6TD,
England.

ISBN 0 904558 77 0

Typeset by Inforum Ltd, Portsmouth, in VIP Baskerville.

Printed and bound by the Pitman Press, Bath.

SAIGA PUBLISHING CO. LTD.
1 Royal Parade, Hindhead, Surrey GU26 6TD,
England.

DEDICATION

To the other six members of the New Set – Peta, Pat, Penny, George, Martin and John, with fond memories of the many happy days we have spent hunting in the Forest. Especially John, for without his continuous encouragement this book would never have been finished.

CONTENTS

Chapter

Note: A Hunting Diary section will be found at the end of each Chapter.

MONOCHROME ILLUSTRATIONS

ACKNOWLEDGEMENTS

The writing of this history has involved a great deal of research over a period of some fourteen months. My first and greatest debt is to the archivists at the Hampshire Record Office in Winchester, especially Mrs Baddage, for it was she who turned what was initially a mere personal curiosity into a realisation that there was perhaps sufficient information available to compile a history.

The following people have also been of tremendous help in one way or another and I would like to record my deep gratitude to them for the way in which they have reacted to my requests for information or assistance: Colonel G. East; Mr J. East; Mr & Mrs Forbes-Smith of 'The Vyne'; Lady Heathcote; Mr & Mrs R.F. Hill; Miss P. Hunt; Mr F. Pearson M.F.H.; Mr A. Rickman; Sir Richard N. Rycroft; Miss J. Skew; Mr George Whitehead; Wing Cmdr. Wood of 'Montacute House'; and the Vicar of St. Mary's Church, Eling.

The following not only generously gave their time but gave me access to, and in some cases loaned me, pictorial material: Mr Maldwin Drummond of 'Cadland House', and his secretary Mrs R. Hendey who helped me find my way through the Drummond family archives; Mr & Mrs P.J.P. Green for permission to use paintings owned by them as plates; Miss R. Pulteney; Mrs P. DuPré; and Mr Michael Clayton of *Horse & Hound* who allowed me to spend a memorable day ploughing through all the back copies of *Horse & Hound*. Mr Clayton has also kindly given permission for those articles by "Dragon" and "St. George" to be reprinted in the various Hunting Diary sections.

AUTHOR'S NOTE

Hunting has been a tradition in the New Forest for 900 years. The first records of foxhunting appear to be in 1675 and from that date onwards scores of packs either visited the Forest, or sprang up, resident in the Forest, in order to hunt the fox rather than the ancient royal quarry, the deer.

However, my task here has been to trace the history back from the present day to the earliest **unbroken** record of hunting the fox, and without doubt this goes back to 1781 when the existing New Forest Hounds, known at that time as "Mr Gilberts Hounds", developed. This pack hunted prior to 1781 but in an informal manner and without a huntsman or regular followers.

When I began my research my intention was purely to find out, for personal reasons of curiosity, how the Hunt started. I did not start to write the history as a book until December 1978 when I borrowed a friend's cottage in Racecourse View, Lyndhurst, for the season. I was, therefore, intrigued to learn, only a week or so before finishing the last chapter, that C.R. Acton, who wrote *Sports & Sportsmen in the New Forest* (1936), which touches on the same subject, had lived in the cottage next-door-but-one.

Although the writing of this book has involved many hours of research, some drawing a disconsolate and often dusty blank, I can honestly say that I have enjoyed every moment that I have spent. It has been a labour of love and I have discovered and learned many fascinating snippets of information — not all of which can be recorded in this book. It was a great pity that the bulk of the records of the Hunt were lost during World War II, but fortunately those families who played such a major part in keeping the Hunt going through two centuries preserved their own records, in particular the Drummonds, the Comptons and the Heathcotes.

Mary S. Lovell

Testbourne,
Hampshire.

Frontispiece **The Chase**

1

The Founder of the New Forest Hunt

1781–1798

Figure 1.1 The Founder

From left to right: Rev'd S. Heathcote; Vincent Hawkins Gilbert, M.F.H., founder of the New Forest Hounds; Sir William Heathcote.

Taken from a painting by Gardinder, c. 1786. The original being the property of the National Trust, held at Montacute House, Somerset, with whose kind permission it is reproduced here.

(*Photo*: B.S. Evans, Yeovil)

CHAPTER 1

The Founder of the New Forest Hunt

1781–1798

EARLY DAYS

Vincent Hawkins Gilbert was born in 1753, the only child of Edward and Mary Gilbert of 'Lambs Corner', Bartley, in the New Forest.

Vincent's mother died before he was three years old and he grew up in an entirely masculine environment. His father was a bluff, hard riding, hard living country squire, inordinately proud of his distant family connection with the powerful Heathcote family of Hursley. In fact, as far as Edward was concerned, the world began and ended at the borders of the New Forest.

His time appears to have been given up almost exclusively to following sporting pursuits. At one time he kept his own pack of harriers, he rode his own horses at the annual race-meeting held at Lyndhurst and hunted often with Sir Phillip Jennings-Clarke's deerhounds, Mr Grove's foxhounds and the many other packs that either lived in or visited the Forest. Growing up in this atmosphere it is hardly surprising that Vincent thought of nothing but foxhunting. Even as a boy he was known as a bold rider to hounds.

YOUTHFUL INTERESTS

After leaving Oxford, he seems to have spent a great deal of his time hunting in Leicestershire with his particular friends Andrew Berkeley Drummond and John Compton. Out of the hunting season these three young men spent their energies driving, horse-racing and following all those sporting activities that were entirely irresistible to young gentlemen of that time.

In June 1778 Vincent was abroad with Mr Drummond when the news of his father's sudden death reached him. He returned home at once, heir to a comfortable estate at the age of only twenty-six years. This estate consisted of lands and properties at Bartley, Milton, Nether Wallop, Sway and Arnewood in Hampshire, plus a small farm in Freshwater, Isle of Wight.

'Lambs Corner', now known as 'Bartley Manor', was the residence of the Gilbert family, and on this site Edward had caused to be built an attractive manor house, which was unfortunately not quite completed when he died. The house was not much to Vincent's immediate taste, however, and he made his home in the comfortable old farmhouse, situated a short distance away, in which he had grown up.

HIS FIRST HOUNDS

He had inherited a few couples of hounds from his father and he purchased a pack from Mr Pole of Dibden. These, together with other sundry purchases, formed his pack of thirty-eight or forty couples. He set up an enviable stud of hunters and driving horses, numbering something above twenty horses, and although at this time he still travelled to Melton for his formal hunting amusement, whenever he was at 'Lambs Corner', Mr Gilbert's pack went out on two or three days a week.

The situation in the Forest at this time was that there were several packs in evidence all of which hunted informally as and when they wished. This obviously caused a certain amount of confusion for the following notice appeared . . .

ADVERTISEMENT

NO HOUNDS ARE TO BE PERMITTED **to hunt in the Forest, except the Lord Warden's, and the Duke of Richmonds (if he should care to come), but in the month of April, viz. from the 1st to the 30th, both days inclusive.**

That no pack be suffered to go out more than three times in one week, and no hounds to be taken out on the intermediate days— and to prevent confusion, it is agreed that the Lord Warden's hounds are to hunt Tuesday, Thursday and Saturday, and no more than two packs of hounds to be in the Forest at the same time.

(It is necessary to remark that the Duke of Richmond had liberty from the preceding Lord Warden to bring his hounds, which was continued to him by the Duke of Gloucester, and he was the only person who had permission to use, not only the kennels and stables, but the King's House likewise, if his Grace should choose to come, which is very improbable.) Then, any strange pack must give way for a time, that there may not be more than two packs at one time.

The earths not to be stopt till half-past four in the morning, and no hounds to be thrown off till five.

The earths during the month of April, not to be stopt but by the Keepers and their servants.

The Keepers have orders not to suffer any fires to be lighted on the earths, or any person to stand on the earths to keep out foxes.

No Tarriers* to be taken out, or Foxes dug, in the month of April.

(A. Cunningham, printer,
opposite the Market House, Southampton).

THE FORMAL HUNT CREATED

In January 1781 we have the first record of Mr Gilbert's hounds hunting the Forest in an organised and formal manner with regular followers. According to Mr Gilbert's diary, a professional huntsman, Woods, was engaged on 7th January, 1781.

From all accounts Woods was not an immediate success and Mr Gilbert discharged him in June of that year for neglecting hounds. In fact, although his domestic arrangements were bleak, Gilbert had a penchant for order, efficiency and style in his kennels and stables, and would suffer no sloppiness. In October that year, however, the diary records that Woods had been "taken on" again, having made proper submission and asked pardon.

*Terriers

Woods was a small and rather dirty man, "but very clever in a run, he rode lop-sided, with one spur digging into his chestnut stallion's side, and swearing the whole time". He remained with Mr Gilbert for nine years, although apparently they did not always see eye to eye, for Mr Gilbert recorded in March 1790 that "the fox was lost by Woods's obstinacy".

In a local guide book written at this time there is the following note: "A noble pack of hounds kept by Vincent Hawkins Gilbert, Esquire, in the bosom of the forest, and designed for the healthy and manly pursuit of the Fox, enables the local gentlemen with frequency, to indulge in this, their favourite amusement".[1*]

GROWING REPUTATION

By 1783 he had a large and regular following of local sportsmen and had begun to earn a growing reputation for his hunting methods, and the sport his hounds showed. The great Peter Beckford visited and expressed his approval of the kennels establishment. Of Beckford it was said: "Never had the Fox nor Hare the honour of being chased to death by so accomplished a hunter, nor huntsmans dinner graced by such urbanity and wit. He can bag a fox in Greek, find a hare in Latin, inspect his kennels in Italian and direct the economy of his stables in exquisite French".[2]

Beckford had hunted often with Mr Gilbert's hounds since 1778 and on a number of occasions the pack had visited Beckford's home at Cranbourne to hunt there. According to several contemporary sources Mr Gilbert is one of the friends referred to often in his celebrated book *Thoughts on Hunting*, although he does not actually name him. "An acquaintance of mine" he wrote, "a good sportsman, but a warm man when he sees the company pressing too closely upon his hounds, begins by crying out, as loudly as he can, 'Hold Hard!'. If anyone should persist after that, he goes on, moderately at first; 'I beg you, sir, you will stop your horse' and 'Pray, sir, stop'. 'Heaven Bless you Sir, stop!' . . . 'Damn your Blood, Sir, stop your horse!'." He also expresses admiration at the excellence of Mr Gilbert's hounds and the scientific manner in which the kennels were managed and administered.

The kennels were at 'Northerwood', at that time owned by Sir Phillip Jennings-Clarke, who had recently given up his own hounds thereby leaving the kennels vacant. Hounds sometimes spent the night at Mr Gilbert's house however, presumably for convenience when there was an especially early start.

HIS LIFE STYLE

An amusing account of a visit to Mr Gilbert's home is told by a friend, who begins by defending Mr Gilbert's actions in rating the followers: " . . . that he should be tenacious of the laws of the field, however, and anxious that his hounds might have fair play was by no means extraordinary, since they were not only the finest pack that ever fell under my limited observation; but they were generally considered as the **crack** one throughout the South of England".

*See end of chapter for source of quotation.

Figure 1.2 The Quarry

Taken from an old print.

Remarkable as the kennel department of Mr Gilbert's establishment might be, the interior economy of his home at 'Lambs Corner' presented the visitor with a phenomena that put the out-of-doors arrangements out of his mind. "They were, sooth to say, such as I have never seen, before or since, for, as Mr Gilbert was a bachelor, there were none of those nice regularities and indications of a 'well ordered home' visible, for which a man must be indebted exclusively to the care, taste and good feeling of a delicate, affectionate and virtuous woman."

"Though by no means devoid of polish and courtesy", Mr Gilbert preferred to live in an easy going, bachelor establishment, which "could boast none of the elegancies, and very few of the comforts, or conveniences of common civilised life. Not a bell, I apprehend, was to be found under the roof; the only summons to the servants at meal times was the roar of the host; who thundered out the monosyllable **'Jack!'**. This was accompanied by a 'Halloa' sufficient to rouse the slumbering hounds in the adjoining kennel, and excite them to full-cry accompaniment.

"The bed in which I slept had never known a curtain; nor did any shutter, or hanging at my window, protect the occupier from being an object of public curiosity. This, however, was a matter of slight importance, on two accounts: the house, being buried deeply in the recesses of the Forest, stood far removed from the gaze of the inquisitive or impertinent eye; and the hour of rising was sufficiently early to secure the operations of the toilet, from the observation of any curious spectator from without."

Depending on the distance to be hacked to the first draw, a tremendous "Tally Ho", was yelled by one of the whippers-in, under each window, at either three, four or five o'clock in the morning. This was immediately obeyed by the guests for, "within a few minutes the whole party, duly equipped in buckskins, boots and spurs and ready for starting were assembled in the parlour".

Before they left, however, there was a hearty breakfast to be eaten. Mr Gilbert's domestic economies certainly did not extend to his tables or his cellars. On this particular day there was "a lordly round of beef, a goodly gammon; a half dissected goose, this flanked by ale and the cordial bottle, filled with fiery juice to defend against the November chill".

"And", says our correspondent "nor were the 'Nimrods' of whom I speak at all backward, in drawing largely upon those antidotes against bodily ill. **Despatch**, indeed was the watchword. Great was the havoc of the moment and all but miraculous the disappearance of the viands.

"The chase followed, with all the ecstacies and adventures and its glorious run; desperate leaps, hair-breadth escapes and successfull termination, evidenced by poor Reynards brush in the cap of the Huntsman; together with its grievous falls, broken heads, dislocated shoulders, limping hounds and jaded riders."

So home they would go, to dinner which, if anything, outshone the sport, and our account of this visit ends: "The hour of the dinner, would of course be rather uncertain. Come however when it might, the aspect of the substantial repast, and the complexion of the Bacchanalian orgies after it, has, at this period, no parallel in England".[3]

Figure 1.3 *New Forest Jasper* **c. 1796**

From a steel engraving in the author's private collection.

A Hunting Day

About this time Mr Gilbert purchased, among others, a hound puppy named *Jasper* from Lord Egremont, and he began to be called "the most celebrated foxhunter in the South of England". The pack was, at this time, still a private one of course, and the followers consisted of friends, near neighbours and the important landowners in the area. Two or three times a week a mounted servant would make the journey around the country to advise those whom the Master wished to invite where and when the next meet was to be. It was the custom then to meet very early in the day, often leaving the kennels in the dark in order to reach the first cover by daybreak. "We took care to be at the covertside by peep o' day, and we went home again to dinner at one o'clock, and so we got a good long afternoon for drinking", wrote a follower. This was not especially confined to the New Forest, and appears to have been the normal practise of foxhunting at that time.

The hunt servants wore round hunt caps, and long scarlet coats, which could lap over and defend their knees against cold and wet.

MR CHUTE AND *NEW FOREST JASPER*

Amongst regular visitors to the Forest was Mr Chute, the founder of the **Vine Hunt**. He and Mr Gilbert had become firm friends and corresponded regularly on the subject of hounds. Mr Chute always said that *New Forest Jasper* was the "model to which he decided to bring his hounds", and to this end he used this lovely stallion hound so exclusively that he became the chief ancestor of the **Vine Pack.**

Indeed *Jasper* achieved considerable fame during his day. Mr Chute, who was somewhat eccentric, felt that as we humans had our ancestors painted to hang upon our walls, so his hounds ought to have the same pleasure. He therefore had a portrait of *Jasper* painted and hung in the kennels. Although the painting showed the hound to have a perfectly symmetrical body, the head and face show a somewhat whimsical grin. This painting was still in existence at 'The Vyne', Mr Chute's old home, in 1958, but cannot now be traced. On the back of the painting was inscribed the couplet:

"Here, see the glory of an ancient breed,
which urges Foxes to their utmost speed."

THE HUNT CLUB

In Autumn 1783 the **New Forest Hunt Club** was formed of the more important gentlemen followers. As far as I can discover the original intention of the Club was that it should be a dining club. The meetings were initially held at Romsey, twice a year, although I have been unable to confirm exactly where.

The founder members of the Hunt Club were:

Lord Wallingford, Lord Palmerston, Lord Euston, Lord Poulett, and Lord Hinton.

Sir Thomas Tancred, Sir Thomas Heathcote, Sir George Rose, and Sir Phillip Jennings-Clarke.

Figure 1.4 The Toast — "Loyal Foxhunters"

"The New Forest Hunt Club was originally formed as a gentleman's dining club."

From a steel engraving of a famous print in the author's private collection.

Mr Vincent Hawkins Gilbert (Founder)
Mr Henry Compton
Mr John Compton
Mr William Heathcote
Mr Andrew Berkeley Drummond
Mr Pole of Dibden
Mr Grove
Mr Harbin of 'Fritham Lodge'
Mr Warton
Mr Reynolds
Mr Sloane (afterwards Mr Sloane-Stanley)
Mr S. Williams
Mr Eyre
Mr Timson
Mr Foyle
Mr Vivien
Mr Peter Serle of Chilworth
Mr Gale
Mr Brocas
Mr Wyndham of Dinton
Mr Le Broque of Lymington
Mr Fleming
Colonel Heywood, of Rhinefield — the Deputy Ranger under the Duke of Gloucester.

The members of the Hunt Club were entitled to wear the uniform which consisted of a long green, double-breasted jacket, with cut-away tails and a black velvet collar, and six buttons down either side of the front. This was worn with a top hat and top boots. Other gentlemen wore scarlet with a plain collar. The membership subscription to the Hunt Club at this time was 1 guinea per annum.

By now these hounds were clearly the most important and established pack in the Forest, and Mr Gilbert seems to have made some representation to the Lord Warden to regularise the situation regarding the number of packs hunting there. He also entertained to dinner all those gentlemen who were wont to hunt their own foxhounds in the Forest at that time, for "private business discussion" to contain the situation. Perhaps because of Mr Gilbert's representations, or more probably because of the importance of some of the Hunt Club members, in January 1784 the following letter was sent to the owners of the other packs:

Southampton, January 27th, 1784

Sir,

The Keepers and others in the New Forest represented to His Royal Highness, the Duke of Gloucester, the great scarcity of Foxes at present in the country, he thinks it proper to revise some regulations that were agreed to with the Duke of Richmond and Lord Eglinton when they had liberty to bring their hounds in the Forest.

He wishes also to add a little to the regulations, as the necessity appears greater at this time.

> **As your hounds have occasionally been in the Forest, he commands me to send you a copy of the regulations and he hopes, as the Forest Hounds will strictly adhere to them, there will be no objection on your part.**
>
> **THE LORD WARDEN HAS GIVEN HIS NAME TO MR GILBERT'S HOUNDS AND FOR THE FUTURE HE WILL LOOK UPON THEM AS THE ESTABLISHED PACK OF THE COUNTRY, but does not mean to prevent your hounds coming out under the enclosed regulations.**
>
> **I have the honour to be, Sir, etc.**

The letter was sent to a Mr Grove and signed by Colonel Heywood — Deputy Warden, and similar letters went out to Mr Pole of Dibden and young Mr Henry Compton, both of whom hunted small private packs in the Forest.

By giving his name to Mr Gilbert's hounds, he not only formally constituted them "the pack of the country", but entitled the members to wear the Royal Button of the Lord Warden of that date, with the Crown and Stirrup emblem upon it.

The members of the New Forest Hunt Club are privileged to share the wearing of this button with all the keepers and servants of the Crown in the Forest, who wear the Crown Livery. It is the oldest Hunt Button in Hampshire and the most interesting.

The **H.H.** (Hampshire Hunt) button, which is the only other Royal button in Hampshire, was not given until sometime after 1788 by the Prince of Wales.[4*]

His Domestic Affairs

Coincidentally with the formation of the Hunt Club, Mr Gilbert moved into the now completed 'Manor House' at 'Lambs Corner', which had been started by his father. A full staff was recruited and among these was a housekeeper, Miss Rebecca Scott. She was seventeen years old, and Mr Gilbert unaccountably fell head over heels in love with her. He described her dark shining curls and bright eyes as "entrancing".

He was something of a romantic figure himself. Although not much above the average height, some five foot nine or ten, he was powerfully built, well-knit and muscular, with crisply crinkling hair and a ready smile. He was kindly, generous to a fault and possessed of an infinite good humour. He rode boldly, but judiciously, and his friends came from all levels of society.

The two formed a romantic attachment that was to last for the remainder of Mr Gilbert's life — they had eight children, although they were never to marry.

What Rebecca did, however, was to correct to some degree the discomfort of the household and, although 'Lambs Corner' remained always a noisy, laughter-filled house, full of Mr Gilbert's foxhunting cronies, it became less filled with "the wild enjoyment of irregular pleasures"!

In 1786, Henry Compton, the Squire of Minstead, died. He had been a second father to Vincent and the loss was felt most keenly. Only a year later the heir, young Henry also died — his pack of foxhounds, kept at his kennels in Boldre, were left to his brother, Mr John Compton, and these were mainly absorbed into Mr Gilbert's pack.

*See 'Notes' at end of chapter

ROYAL VISITORS

In 1789 the Lord Warden, Prince William of Gloucester visited the Forest, and hunted with the New Forest Hounds, dining afterwards at 'Lambs Corner'.

The same month His Majesty King George III, accompanied by the Prince of Wales, spent a few days at Lyndhurst, staying at the 'King's House'. The handsome young Prince, for in those days he really was Prince Charming, spent two days out with the hounds. He also attended a banquet given by the Hunt Club at 'Northerwood'. Both 'Northerwood' and the 'King's House' were "illuminated" that night and the local populace turned out in flocks to see this wondrous sight. The Prince graciously gave permission for 'Northerwood House' to be called henceforward 'Mount Royal'; however, upon his decease it reverted to its former name.

The King was on a "tour" following his recovery from a serious illness. At the edge of the Forest the royal party were greeted at "Cadenham"*, and the King presented with the traditional gift of the foresters — two white greyhounds, wearing silver collars held by silken cords.

Whilst in the Forest the guard consisted of archers and bowmen, dressed in green. When the King attended church in Lyndhurst the populace insisted on singing "God Save The King" instead of the psalm.

In 1789 or 1790 the meetings of the Hunt Club were transferred to Lyndhurst from Romsey. It seems that at this time the hounds became a subscription pack, for records show that the gentlemen paid 20 guineas a year for the privilege of following Mr Gilbert's hounds. Some of the more important members, however, gave more — Sir William Heathcote, who was Treasurer, subscribed £105 and Mr John Compton £52.10s. Meetings of the Hunt Club were held twice annually at either the 'King's House', or 'Northerwood House' and the Hunt appointed to the position of Honorary Secretary S. Williams, Esquire, of Lyndhurst.

HUNT SERVANTS

In 1791 Woods, the huntsman, left and there is some contention over the reason for this. However, as he went on to the **Belvoir**, where he remained until 1794, one may assume that he was not discharged. He eventually returned to the Forest to retire at Emery Down. He had the reputation of being somewhat miserly, and after his death in 1820 there was a local sensation when his relatives found a hoard of money totalling over £1,000, £39 of which was in silver and believed to be the 'caps' saved over the years. In those days it was the custom to cap the field when there had been a good run and a kill, to show correct appreciation to the hunt servants.

After Woods left, Tull came as huntsman for one season, then Fox for one season and from 1793 onwards, Sebright, who was the father of the much celebrated Tom Sebright who earned a lasting reputation with the **Fitzwilliam Hunt.** Under Sebright the hounds showed brilliant sport. During the season Mr Gilbert hunted each alternate day — Monday, Wednesday and

*Now known as Cadnam.

Figure 1.5 The Forest

Typical New Forest scene.

(*Photo courtesy*: John A. Belcher)

Friday— with only the occasional interruption for weather. However, for the month of April, when Lyndhurst was visited each year by the **Grovely Hunt,** every keen sportsman who had sufficient horses, and was equal to the exertion, hunted, wined and dined on six days out of seven.

Among newspaper reports of the Hunt is the slightly censorious note to the effect that "the appearance of several students from Mr Le Broque's academy at Ashley Hill, Lymington, is not infrequent amongst the red coats to the rear of Mr Gilbert's foxhounds". Mr Le Broque was a keen supporter and no doubt felt that he was merely encouraging manly pursuits!

HIS EARLY DEATH

Towards the end of 1797 Mr Gilbert became ill with a serious stomach disorder. Although he continued to hunt, he was impressed enough by the pain, and his doctor's and friends' concern, to make a will securing the future of Rebecca, and more particularly their eight children on whom he doted.

Advised by his friend and confidant Andrew Berkeley Drummond, the banker, he made a very complicated entail, known as "The Gilbert Trust", to cover his rather unusual domestic affairs. The executors, Sir William Heathcote, Mr Andrew Drummond and Mr Arthur Mist of 'Moyles Court', were entrusted with the care and education of the children and the future of the family.

After Christmas he went with a party to Cheltenham, although in great pain. He died there, suddenly and without fuss, on 27th January, 1798, in the prime of his life — he was only forty-four years old.

His death was an irreparable loss to his enormous circle of friends and indeed "to every sportsman within twenty miles of Lambs Corner". He was a brilliant man, very personable, able and well educated. He had a quiet and gentle wit, which was wont to explode in a series of loud shouts of laughter when he was amused. His untimely death cast a shadow over hunting in the New Forest, which was of course abandoned for the remainder of the season.

His body was brought home for burial, and the funeral took place at St Mary's Church, Eling, on 9th February, 1798.

Mr Compton bought the hounds at the subsequent auction, for an undisclosed price. *The Grey*, Mr Gilbert's favourite horse fetched 60 guineas, the remaining horses in the stable fetched £310.19.6d in total.

The estate was not in good heart, the properties had been neglected and a great deal of the comfortable inheritance left by his father had been spent on the hounds. However, there was sufficient to educate and provide for each of the children, who were to be brought up as gentlefolk, and for Rebecca.

The eldest son, Edward, was heir and he became a leading member of the Hunt in later years as Major 'Jemmy' Gilbert, living at 'Bartley Lodge', Cadnam.

Rebecca was married, less than two years later, to a Mr Bowles. The couple lived at nearby Plaitford and Rebecca raised a second family. The first boy was named Vincent— Mr Bowles it seems, was not of a jealous turn of mind.

It was a tranquil, though happy life according to her children, in total contrast to the noisy, brilliant years spent at 'Lambs Corner' where Vincent Hawkins Gilbert founded a tradition of hunting that was to last until the present day.

Rebecca lived to a ripe old age, dying in 1850, aged 87. She was buried in Plaitford Churchyard.

HUNTING DIARY 1781-1798

Unfortunately there are few recorded runs of this period. It was fashionable merely to record where hounds met, found and where they killed or lost. There is, however, mention of Mr Gilbert's "finest hound hunt".

19th April, 1789

"Hounds found below Burley Beacon, and ran for a full four hours, before accounting for their fox at Hasley Hill." This was not a long point in terms of distance but as hounds ran Mr Gilbert estimated that they covered some 18 miles. "It was", he concludes "the best run I ever saw in the Forest."

Taken from *Sporting Reminiscences of Hampshire*, by "Aesop".

NOTES

1 *A Companion Guide to Lymington* by Richard Warner.
2 Sir Peter Egerton Bridges
3 *Literary Recollections* by Richard Warner
4 **Crown and Stirrup**.

The unusual stirrup on the Hunt Button is that known in the Forest as "Rufus' Stirrup". It has been positively dated as sixteenth century, so unfortunately cannot have belonged to Rufus. It still hangs in the 'Verderers Hall' in Lyndhurst.

It has an interesting history attached to it. In the days when the hunting of deer was a Royal perogative, no-one who lived in the Forest was allowed to keep a dog large enough to chase and pull down a deer. To judge whether a dog fell within this category the animal had to be able to squeeze through this stirrup, which measures some 30 inches around. The unfortunate alternatives facing the owner of a dog who could not comply were a large fine, or the removal of the animal's front toes, so that he could not run.

2

The Early Years

1798–1808

Figure 2.1 Mr John Compton, M.F.H.

Master of the New Forest Hunt from 1800-1803.

Taken from a painting owned by Mr P.J.P. Green, c. 1800.

(*Photo*: John Tarlton)

CHAPTER 2

The Early Years

(1798–1808)

THE SQUIRES OF "THE MANOR"

One of the important founder members of the Hunt was the Squire of Minstead, Mr Henry Compton. He was a contemporary of Mr Gilbert's father and a keen foxhunter. He was also one of the great gentleman jockeys of the day, his racing career spanning thirty-five years during which time his horses ran in 119 races, and he was the owner of the famous *Compton Barb* later known as the *Sedley Grey Arabian*. In the spring of 1776 he acquired a half share in the racehorse *Highflier*, Lord Bolinbroke was the co-owner. *Highflier* was the son of *Herod* — an equally celebrated horse. In 1779, Lord Bolinbroke, finding himself in rather deep water financially to "Old Tatt" (the founder of Tattersalls, Richard Tattersall), sold *Highflier* to him as part of the settlement of accounts. Between 1779 and 1793 the horse was to prove a gold mine to its new owner and earned over £25,000 in prizes and stud fees (he took over from *Eclipse* as a foal getter), in those days a great deal of money. Mr Tattersall named his house near Ely, built from the proceeds of *Highflier's* successes, 'Highflier Hall', and his favourite toast was "the hammer and *Highflier*".

Like Edward Gilbert, Henry Compton had raised his sons, Henry (his heir) and John, to be keen sportsmen. Young Henry, in fact, had his own pack of hounds which he kept kennelled at 'Heywood House' in Boldre.

In addition to being High Sheriff of Hampshire, 'The Squire' was a noted Melton man, spending much of his time in the winter at 'The Old Club' at Melton.

In 1786, as mentioned earlier, Henry died at Bath, aged sixty-seven. He was followed to the churchyard within the year by his eldest son, also named Henry. Young Henry's hounds were left to the surviving son John, and they were in turn presented to Mr Gilbert. Mr John Compton inherited, among other properties, the manor at Minstead. At this time the manor house was a fairly small building and John immediately set about enlarging it, the work being completed in 1792, (this building was demolished in 1949 being replaced by the present 'Minstead Manor'). John also rebuilt the southern transept of Minstead Church in order to provide space for a large, square family pew. In his father's time this area where the Compton family prayed had more resembled a comfortable parlour than anything else, with its fireplace, carpets, sofa and a table in the middle with books on. A family vault was also constructed under the chancel.

It was John Compton who, after the untimely death of his "greatest friend"

Mr Gilbert, saw to it that hunting continued in the Forest. Here was no set of retiring provincials. For within this small circle of gentlemen who formed the Hunt Club at the close of the eighteenth century were government ministers, members of parliament, close friends of "Prinny", and many of the members were noted by the famous "Nimrod" for their riding ability in the fast and furious 'Shires'. John Compton was also High Sheriff of Hampshire.

It appears that in November 1798 the Hunt Club members met at Lyndhurst and it was decided that there were sufficient gentlemen who were interested in continuing to maintain a pack of hounds to hunt the Forest. The Secretary had especially planned the date so that members would have received their 'Michaelmas Rents' and would, therefore, be in a position to pay their subscriptions at the meeting. It will be remembered that the subscription was 20 guineas — a goodly sum in those days!

So, hunting in the Forest continued for two years under the management of John Compton, Esquire, aided by Sir William Heathcote, Hon. Treasurer, and Mr S. Williams, Hon. Secretary. Mr Drummond also played a major part in the management of the country during this period. Sebright remained as huntsman.

In 1800 John Compton became Master. This was a logical outcome as he owned the hounds anyway, and had been largely responsible for the hunting arrangements for the previous two years. The hounds remained kennelled at 'Northerwood House', ably cared for by Tom Sebright, a "quiet, kindly soul" who, according to "Druid", a celebrated contemporary writer, was "quite a huntsman worthy in his day, and showed all the science of a master forester when he hunted the New Forest. Nearly to the last (he died in his eighty-sixth year), he would trot out on his pony".

In 1803 Mr Compton died suddenly, aged only fifty-three, leaving a fourteen year old son, Henry Coombe Compton, as heir to the Compton estates. His wife survived him only a matter of months, leaving Henry the ward of Andrew Berkeley Drummond.

Andrew Berkeley Drummond

Local foxhunting has good reason to be grateful to Mr Drummond for he was a founder member and staunch supporter of the New Forest Hunt Club. He was a great "preserver" of foxes on his own estate at 'Cadlands', and the amount of work that he expended on behalf of the Hunt was enormous. He was, indeed, an early version of what is now known as a "business tycoon", for he was a member of the Drummond banking family, and in addition to his activities in the Forest ran the bank at Charing Cross.

He was the joint guardian of the eight Gilbert children as well as young master Compton. All the boys in his care grew up to be keen sportsmen, as indeed did his own sons. It was certainly Mr Drummond who once again rallied the members again after this second blow, and organised the continuity of sport in the Forest.

Henry Coombe Compton

Incidently, it was Henry Coombe Compton who, in subsequent years, provided the Hunt with the site for the present kennels at 'Furzey Lawn', in

Figure 2.2 The Meet

From a steel engraving, c. 1803, in the author's private collection.

(Author's note: This is not the N.F.H. — I believe it to be the King's Staghounds, but, in any case, it is a typical hunting scene of the period. The gentlemen are wearing the black neckcloth rather than the now familiar hunting tie in white.)

1844. There is a rather amusing, if slightly ribald anecdote, told about him in later life. It concerns his great friend, the Earl of Errol, who lived at 'Rosiere', a villa near the lovely old manor of 'Cuffnells', outside Lyndhurst. It appears that in 1819 his Lordship died in the most reduced circumstances, and upon his being summoned to the house Mr Compton found it besieged with the Earl's creditors and the entire situation was most unpleasant. He discharged the creditors and had the body tenderly removed to the 'Manor House', where it lay in mournful state for some days, in charge of four devoted retainers. The night before the funeral, Mr Compton was awakened by an uproar coming from the dining room, and upon investigation found to his horror the four faithful retainers in an advanced state of intoxication, throwing dice on the coffin lid! He kicked them out into the night in his slippered feet, causing him some discomfort but much satisfaction. The body was interred eventually in Minstead Church, where the Errol hatchment still hangs.

Another interesting fact is that through his marriage to Charlotte Mills of Bisterne, a direct descendant of Edward III through Lady Anne Plantagenet, Henry's sons and grandsons became entitled to quarter the Royal Arms. They could also trace a close relationship to George Washington, President of the United States of America.

THE "ALL THE TALENTS" COMMITTEE

The season that began in October 1803 found a difficult situation. No-one felt able to take on the Mastership, although there was no lack of keen supporters. Eventually it was decided to manage the Hunt by committee. This committee consisted of Lord Cavan, of Eaglehurst; Mr Charles Mitchell and Mr S. Williams. They retained old Tom Sebright as huntsman. This committee were later known as "All the Talents", a nickname they shared with a coalition government of the day!

Lord Cavan was a military celebrity. He had attained the rank of Major General in 1798, having joined the Coldstream Guards as an ensign in 1779. He was wounded at Valenciennes in 1793 and commanded a line brigade in Ireland, 1798-99, and then in Egypt until 1803. This latter brigade was sent to attack the western flank of Alexandria, and the city surrendered on 2nd September, 1801. He was then left in command of the entire army remaining in Egypt. He held a Brigade Command during the invasion alarms of 1803-5 and then became Lt. Gen., commanding the Isle of Wight. He was one of six officers, besides Lord Nelson, who received the Diamond Aigrette as Knight of the Crescent, and later became the Governor of Calshot Castle.

I can find no history for Mr Mitchell. Mr Williams, it will be recalled, had served as Honorary Secretary for some years. His wife is the first lady, that I can find any record of, riding to these hounds.[1]

Sir George Rose

One of the leading members of the Hunt during this period was Sir George Rose who was Lord Chancellor in the government of William Pitt.

He lived at 'Cuffnells' which was, according to a contemporary source, the most beautifully appointed and furnished house in the area, and was honoured by visits from their Majesties King George III and Queen Charlotte who stayed there on their way to Weymouth, it being a favourite "watering place". Their host, although fully conscious of the honour, found himself often embarrassed and upset by His Majesties continuous derogatory references to the Prince of Wales.

Sir George was a very public spirited man. When he died, his funeral was held at Lyndhurst and the service was read by the Rev. F. Compton. At the end of the service the church doors were locked and the congregation were informed of a codicil to Sir George's will. This was that every male person present would receive the sum of 10 shillings upon leaving the church, provided they thought it worthwhile to accept. As the *Hampshire Chronicle* recorded: "Doubtless, many others, had they known, would have made their attendance, that day!".

In 1808 at the end of spring hunting, it was decided to accept the offer of Mr John Warde to hunt the country. He was probably one of the most famous foxhunters ever, and certainly of his day. Tom Sebright was ready to retire anyway, and the committee were more than happy to make way for the new Master.

HUNTING DIARY 1798-1808

"Hunting in the New Forest, in the month of April, is charming beyond description. A bright gaudy day is not supposed, generally, to be favourable for hunting, but in the New Forest in the spring it cannot be too brilliant. In fact, in wet weather they can do nothing. In 1802 we hunted 13 days in April, and perhaps the 1st or 2nd of May, and killed eleven foxes after a run. Not the sort of run you have in Leicestershire of 10 or 12 miles from point to point, but to a man who loves hunting it is inconceivably beautiful. With good health, youth on your side, pink and leathers in good trim and a pleasant nag, nothing could be more enchanting or heart stirring than a meet in the New Forest on a lovely morning.

"The bogs in that country extend for miles and if you get in you will never get out again, at least with your horse. Here the foxes delight to lie, and seeing them draw up to him is one of the most delicious sensations imaginable. They go with their heads up, sniffing the breeze, and show you he is there though they can't speak to him. At length you hear a tongue, then another and another until the sweet melody enraptures your senses and drives all cares away. There was no driving 'em over the line, as is now the case but the local sportsmen knew when they were on the scent and when off it. They had not more than eighteen couples of effective hounds, but they were the cream of the cream. Old Tom* knew the Forest well, and showed the hand of a master there. The hounds were mainly descended from a good hound bred by Lord Egremont, called *Jasper*, who was a model of a foxhound both in shape and work.

"In those days there was a Hunt Club at the King's House at Lyndhurst, where there was a jovial party, good cheer and, to a lover of hunting, the month of April was altogether a month of pleasure without alloy."

Taken from *Post and Paddock* by "Druid".

*Old Tom — Tom Sebright, huntsman to the N.F.H. from 1793—1808

NOTE

1 *Annals of Sport*: "Mrs Williams can be seen often, well up with these hounds, dressed in a neat Forest Green habit."

3

The Father of Foxhunting

1808–1813

Figure 3.1 Mr John Warde, M.F.H.

Master of the New Forest Hunt from 1808-1814.

This engraving is after a famous portrait by James Green, R.A., and was to have included two favourite hounds, *Glory* and *Beauty*. Unfortunately, *Beauty* died just before the sittings began and Mr Warde claimed that he is depicted saying: "Though my *Beauty* has departed, my *Glory* remains".

(*Photo*: Brian Manby)

CHAPTER 3

The Father of Foxhunting

1803–1813

PREVIOUS MASTERSHIPS

The most celebrated Master of the New Forest Hounds was **Mr John Warde**; known variously as "Father of the Field", "Glorious John Warde" and more often "the Father of Foxhunting".

He was born at Squerries, Kent, in 1752 into the easy life of a wealthy, sporting, country family. From a very early age he showed an intense aptitude for the science of venery, and was one of the first Masters of hounds to advocate travelling from country to country to gain experience of hunting in diverse conditions.

Certainly he hunted a pack of foxhounds in France in 1773 when he was only twenty-one years old. Upon returning to England he hunted in Westerham, Kent, around his family estate and the neighbourhood with his own pack until 1776. He then went to Berkshire for four years followed by Oxfordshire and Warwickshire. In 1797 he assumed Mastership of the **Pytchley Hunt** where his fame spread rapidly on account of the excellent sport his hounds showed. In 1808 he sold the Pytchley pack to Lord Althorp for 1,000 guineas, retaining a few of the bitches and young hounds. With these, together with a small number he purchased from the retiring Master of the **Thurlow Hunt,** he travelled south to take Mastership of the New Forest.

Personality

He had a striking personality, a well developed sense of humour, and a ready wit. He was welcomed by the New Forest sportsmen to a man, and so began a most successful reign of six years. His knowledge of hunting science, and his opinions on the breeding and management of hounds was much respected, and he was not tolerant of anyone who voiced disagreement with his theories; obviously he felt that his successful track record was sufficient support to these. Once, when seeing a whip taking liberties with a horse he made him get off and run for the rest of the day!

He was something of a gourmet; "Never refuse a good dinner *from* home, unless you have a better one *at* home", was his advice, and this was obviously the source of his weight problem. He had substantial girth and weighed over 17 stone and so finding suitable horses became an acute anxiety to him, especially since he was not a rich man. He wrote to a wealthy friend: "Our weight is differently situated, yours being in your pocket where I am so very light".

He was most fortunate in having a wife, his beloved Susanna, who was very sympathetic to her husband's addiction to foxhunting and once, when he had almost decided he must give up hounds, she emphatically advised him not to, telling him that things would surely improve and then he would regret his action. He took her advice and continued, hoping that she was right, and two weeks later received word from his banker that a sum of £1,000 had been credited anonymously to his account, by a "friend to foxhunting". It was many years before he was to discover that the 'friend' was none other than his wife. She was in possession of a private fortune which, unusually for those days, was in her own power.

HIS HOUNDS AND HUNT SERVANTS

The pack he bred, which hunted the country so admirably, caused much amusement and joking in the hunting world generally. Like the pack he had hunted at the **Pytchley** — dubbed by the ageing Hugo Meynell of the **Quorn** as "John Wardes Jackasses" — they were larger than the contemporary fashion, one stallion hound measuring 27 inches. In spite of his sense of humour, Meynell's remarks touched him on the raw. He cared passionately for his theories, and for his hounds, and his way of answering the sneers was to purchase a couple of the **Quorn** draft — the worst possible, ugly, difficult animals. He named then *Queer'un* and *Quornite* and was happy to point them out as being typical **'Shire'** types, which of course they were not!

He had the last laugh, however, for all his hounds were outstanding for their steadiness, nose, voice and perseverence. He called them his "darlings" and put an individual value on each one.

Indeed, they were in great demand, and many of the best huntsmen in England were glad to get the blood. Certainly some of our most famous packs strain back to them and it is now accepted that the breeding of such large hounds, with great ribs and fine bone was of service to the modern fox-hound. He kennelled the hounds firstly at 'King's House' and later removed them to his home, 'Foxlease'.

He brought with him Abbey, his huntsman, who had previously been with Colonel John Cooke at the **Hambledon**. He also brought Will Neverd and Zach Goddard as his whippers-in. All these servants went on to make names for themselves in foxhunting history. They were principally notable, however, because they had served the great John Warde.

Neverd was quickly appraised as "a first rate man", quiet in the field, civil to everyone and with a wonderful nerve for riding to hounds. He later became a renowned huntsman elsewhere; his career spanning over forty years.

Goddard was immortalised by the "Druid", in his fascinating series of books on the subjects of the Turf and the Chase. He refers to him fondly as "Old Zach; the varmint". Zach was only 5-foot, 6 inches and never weighed much above 9 stone and someone once said to John Warde, "If I had hounds I should want all my men to be like Zach".

"Oh you should eh?", answered the Master, "Fond of lightweights are you? Well I don't know any difference between lightweights and heavyweights except that one breaks their backs and the other their hearts!".

Zach's "Holloa" was almost unearthly in its shrillness and he always used it

Figure 3.2 The South-West of England — a guide to the position of hunts.

in preference to the horn when he became huntsman for "it carried further". As an old man he was fond of telling how, in his early days in the Forest, John Warde would come pounding on the door at three in the morning for cubhunting. The men slept over the stable and they could hear the Master yelling at them "to come and give those foxes a touch". "But", said Old Zach "we never stirred less'n he persevered and came at the door a second time".

BLUE RUIN

In spite of his great weight, Warde was a good rider, and rode fast and well. He was as fond of horses as he was of hounds. He came upon his renowned horse *Blue Ruin* pulling a brewers cart in Newbury market place and lost no time in buying the plucky youngster. The blue roan had been bred by a gin distiller, by a thoroughbred sire out of a half bred mare. The name came from his colour and his origins in the gin trade. John Warde received many offers, which became increasingly lavish over the years, for the gallant animal, but none were ever considered. Thomas Ashetton Smith said after riding him, "I was never better carried in my life"[2] and offered to buy him, but even his offer was declined.

Blue Ruin carried his bulky owner invincibly to hounds and, in addition, was a favourite driving horse. Second only to hunting, Warde's other interest in life was driving. He was a leading member of the **Bensington Driving Club**, one of the early four-in-hand clubs to which every budding whipster aspired.

There is a famous Webb engraving of Mr Warde on *Blue Ruin*, with a favourite hound, *Betsy*, by W. Barraud.

This engraving which appeared in the *New Sporting Magazine* in 1831 records that *Blue Ruin* "did 62 miles in a curricle without the bridle taken from his mouth". There are many stories of Mr Warde's witty sayings and "Aesop" records that he "revelled in jokes and jests, and being always cheery himself had the happy knack of making everybody about him cheerful". There was a gentleman of very large fortune residing in the New Forest when he hunted it, and no-one was ever invited to partake of his hospitality. Mr Warde declared that he would get a dinner or, at any rate, **something** to eat or drink at his house: One day this gentleman returned from hunting before the hounds had found, as it was late before they did so, and a capital run they had, killing their fox. On their way home they passed this gentleman's house, John Warde stopped and rang the bell. The footman who answered it said 'his master was at dinner'. 'Never mind, I must see him to tell him of the splendid run we had.' He was shown into the dining-room where this unhospitable gentleman was dining with three servants waiting on him. John Warde described the run and regretted that the other had not remained, but although he went over the run two or three times he was not asked to take anything. At last, giving it up in despair, he wished him good night; but, just as he got to the door, he turned round and said 'Will you allow your footman to bring me a glass of small beer?'."[3]

Every Monday evening for many years his portly form could be seen at dinner at the house of Mr Richard Tattersall (the son of "Old Tatt") in North Hampshire. The room was in keeping with the company. Portraits of *Highflier*, Old Tatt and Mr Richard Tattersall on his lovely bay, *Bonaparte*, looking

Figure 3.3 *Blue Ruin*

John Warde Esq. on his faithful horse, *Blue Ruin*, with a favourite hound, *Betsy*, c. 1810.

From a steel engraving in the author's private collection.

down on the assembled company of sportsmen from the walls.

The **Doncaster Cup**, won by *Crookshanks* in 1781, always held the punch. The pipe of port, which the host laid down annually had a heavy tax upon it for each man had to drink to "John Warde and the Noble Science", from a silver foxhead which held nearly a pint. None stood the process better than "glorious John" himself, and he would rise from the table as steady as a rock, in the short hours, and never leave till he had gone up to the drawing room to bid Mrs Tattersall goodbye.

The Derby Dinner held annually would have seemed as nothing without him to represent foxhunting and "true as the dial to the sun, he would, a few minutes before six, issue from his yellow charriot, in his silver knee and shoe buckles". His servants wore that same style of low-crowned hat, which the *Blue Ruin* and *Betsy* picture has imortalized and their brown coats were edged with silver braid. A large cold game pie held pride of place at the feast, and the host especially prided himself on the Rhenish hock which some foreign friends sent him. The venison was from Goodwood. No host held the party together better or told such old fashioned stories from behind his stiff white choker, and it was only when his memory failed, and his jokes would not come out so crisp and neat as of yore, that he reluctantly gave it up.

NIMROD'S REPORT

Writing of Mr Warde as a sportsman in 1824 some years after he had left the Forest, "Nimrod" says, "I met Mr Warde's hounds again in the neighbourhood of Newbury. When mounted on his hunter, and in the midst of his hounds, I could not help looking at him with admiration, when I considered that I had before me a man whose long life had been devoted to foxhunting, and whose character as a sportsman had always stood so high; whose name is every day quoted as authority for some rule of conduct in the kennel, or as the author of some witty saying or pleasant joke; and, as I before observed, as a real sample of old English blood. My brother sportsmen will be happy to hear that he looks in high health and vigour, as a proof of which I was told that, being president of his club a short time since, and having, to use the words of my informant, 'screwed up his party almost to the top hole', he pulled a fox's head out of his pocket and drank a bumper to foxhunting. I know not what weight Mr Warde now rides, but I do not wonder at his telling a gentleman who was out with him that it would be the *best recipe for his hot horse*. He reminded me of a celebrated welter weight in the Forest, who, on being asked what he weighed, replied that he was *'two-and-twenty stone on the weighbridge'* — as much as to say 'no scales will hold me'."

HIS RESIGNATION

In summer 1814 catastrophe struck. Hound madness broke out in the kennels and Warde lost forty couples. Dispirited he resigned his Mastership of the New Forest and with the few hounds he saved moved to the **Craven**. Upon being asked by a Hunt Club committee member the nature of the 'boundaries' of the **Craven,** he replied "it is a simple triangle, bordered by London, Oxford and Bath".

In all he was Master of Foxhounds for over fifty years, dying in his London house aged eighty-six in 1838. *Blue Ruin* had an almost equal record of longevity — he lived to be thirty.

SOME OF THE RECORDED SAYINGS OF JOHN WARDE ESQ.

Upon Horses:

"Half the goodness of a horse goes in at his mouth."

"Never buy a horse from a rich man who hunts, nor from a poor man, until you have tried him."

"Never believe a word any man says about a horse he wishes to sell — not even a Bishop!"

"Do not trespass too far on the willing powers of your horses. Hundreds of good hunters have been destroyed by the neglect of a mere act of humanity towards exhausted nature in a noble and willing animal."

Upon Hounds:

"Breed your hounds with bone and nose: without the one they will tire; without the other become slack."

"Who would draft *good* **hounds?"**

"I have had hundreds of *beautiful* **hounds who were not worth one day's meal. Indeed it sometimes strikes me that, as hounds improve in beauty, which they certainly do, they lose other more necessary qualities."**

"I have found large hounds suit all countries, which small ones do not and they are generally more docile than small ones."

"Hounds, like horses, must be fit to go, or good foxes will beat them."

Upon Servants:

"Never keep a drinking man, nor a very pretty maid-servant."

**"Dear Sir,
If J. B —— had been worth keeping I should not have parted with him.
Yours truly,
J. Warde"**

"I like to see a huntsman alive and stirring as well as his hounds, when he enters a covert to draw for his fox."

"There is certainly something very cheering to the field in the 'cheering halloa' of a huntsman."

Upon the New Forest:

"I never knew the nature of a bog, till I went to Hampshire I saw a good hat on top of one, and there was a head in it, and the head said, 'I don't care for myself, but do help to get my horse up, he's in the bog below'."

NEW FOREST HUNT POEMS 1

The New Forest Hunt by S. Nicoll, 1810

NEW FOREST HUNT

**November the nineteenth, despising the weather
Some sportsmen of Dibden assembled together;
After waiting awhile for John Warde and his hounds
They were quieted at once by the heart-stirring sounds
Of "Try for — Yoi! Wind him! Creep up to him, boys,"
Hush! Hush! We shall head him; don't made such a noise
Now observe how they draw! Look at Spinster, the jade —
Like lightning she's joined by the rest of the pack,
"Tally ho! Gone away!" is hollered by Zach.[2]
Then over the road, 'cross the main earth he breaks
And by Sir John Keane's house the enclosure he takes,
And Ipley Farm bridge the first point that he makes,
But here headed, he turned up the lane thro' the flood
Running over the bottom for Langley Great Wood.
Here he's headed again, but not dreaming on death
He now gallantly faces the wide open heath.
When riding and hollering, elated with joy,
To the right we leave Matley, to the left the Decoy;
At the very best pace up the hill we ascend
And run straight o'er the open to Denny Lane end,
To the right of the Lodge, thro' Etherise flying,
On entering Woodfidley we thought he was dying.
But still onward again the hounds eagerly push
And pass through at top speed, the enclosure Blackbush.
Here the veteran Bos[3] never minding his neck
By his riding too hard, brought the hounds to a check
But Solon, esteemed the most excellent hound,
By his shrill squeaking tongue made the cover resound,
And others quick join him, like pigeons in flight
For when Solon speaks to it he's sure to be right.
Away forward they strain to Whitley Lodge plain
When old Farmer New reynard's headed again
And reluctantly forced, being pressed by the pack,
To retrace in a circle the same country back,
And still farther yet, his heart never failing,
He makes for the corner of Pickering's pailing,
Turning up to the left reaching Ramnor's great hill,
The hounds get behind, tho' assisted by Will.
Just here with hard riding the horses were spent,
And the pack shortly brought to a cold hunting scent,
But that's nothing to them, for what's seldom the case,
They can hunt a low scent and yet run the best pace.
With hounds that in hunting so brilliantly shine,
Such as Alfred and Hotspur, he still kept his line.
While slowly advancing Zachariah cries "Hark!"
He's now hollered again right away to New Park.
Then away to the holloa we instantly trot
And with eagerness ask if he's "hunted" or not.
"Quite done," was replied, "and he shortly must tire,
For his tongue's hanging out, and he's covered with mire."
With fair scent through the Park we proceed**

And keep gaining upon him quite up to Queen Mead.
Across Over Green Flat, now he's pressed by the hounds,
Straight away for the corner of Brockenhurst Grounds.
The pack here he hoped by his cunning to bother,
Up one side the hedge, down the ditch on the other.
By this shifting and dodging we thought him our own
But away to Rhinefield Alfred tells us he's gone.
Through the vile yew enclosures (some more of the sort
When planned by Glenberrie, will ruin our sport.
Let me tell the wise lord, if not too affronting,
They will ruin the public as well as the hunting).
But I'm now off my scent, so I'll quickly hark back
And leave this dull lord to return to the pack.
To the left up the bottom like lightning they fled,
As they stream up the hill "only see what a head!"
Was exclaimed by John Warde, "Now again how they press
Sure no hounds in the kingdom such powers possess."
Here no man could tell which hound worked the most
As they strove all alike towards Wilverley Post.
But not liking the open, he turned for some gorse,
When the hounds were again overrode by old Bos.
Though this error my friend commits in the field
For hard riding and keenness to no man he'll yield.
Now they hit it once more into Hinchelsea break
And stout as the day, made the whole cover shake.
Sure alas! at this sport was misfortune our guide
For with friend we observe the whole pack to divide —
On different scents — some went this way, some that,
Some ascending the hill, some crossing the flat.
From this direful disaster we found it in vain
To recover the scent of our old friend again.
Thus finished a chase of three hours or more,
Such a chase as scarce ever I witnessed before.
Then homeward we walked as but few chose to trot,
For almost all the horses their gruel had got.
Now snug in my cottage, of good generous port,
A full bumper I drink to John Warde and the sport.
Then the Balls and the Routs of Southampton remove
'Tis of port and good humour we sportsmen approve.
May to Lyndhurst repair some more friends of the chase
And tea and the Tabbies be banished the place!

Notes

1 S. Nichols, the author, was subsequently Master of N.F.H. from 1814-1828.
2 Zach Goddard
3 Mr Boscowan, a regular rider to these hounds.

Figure 3.4 Foxhounds in Full Cry

From an engraving in the author's collection.

4

Sam Nicolls

1814–1828

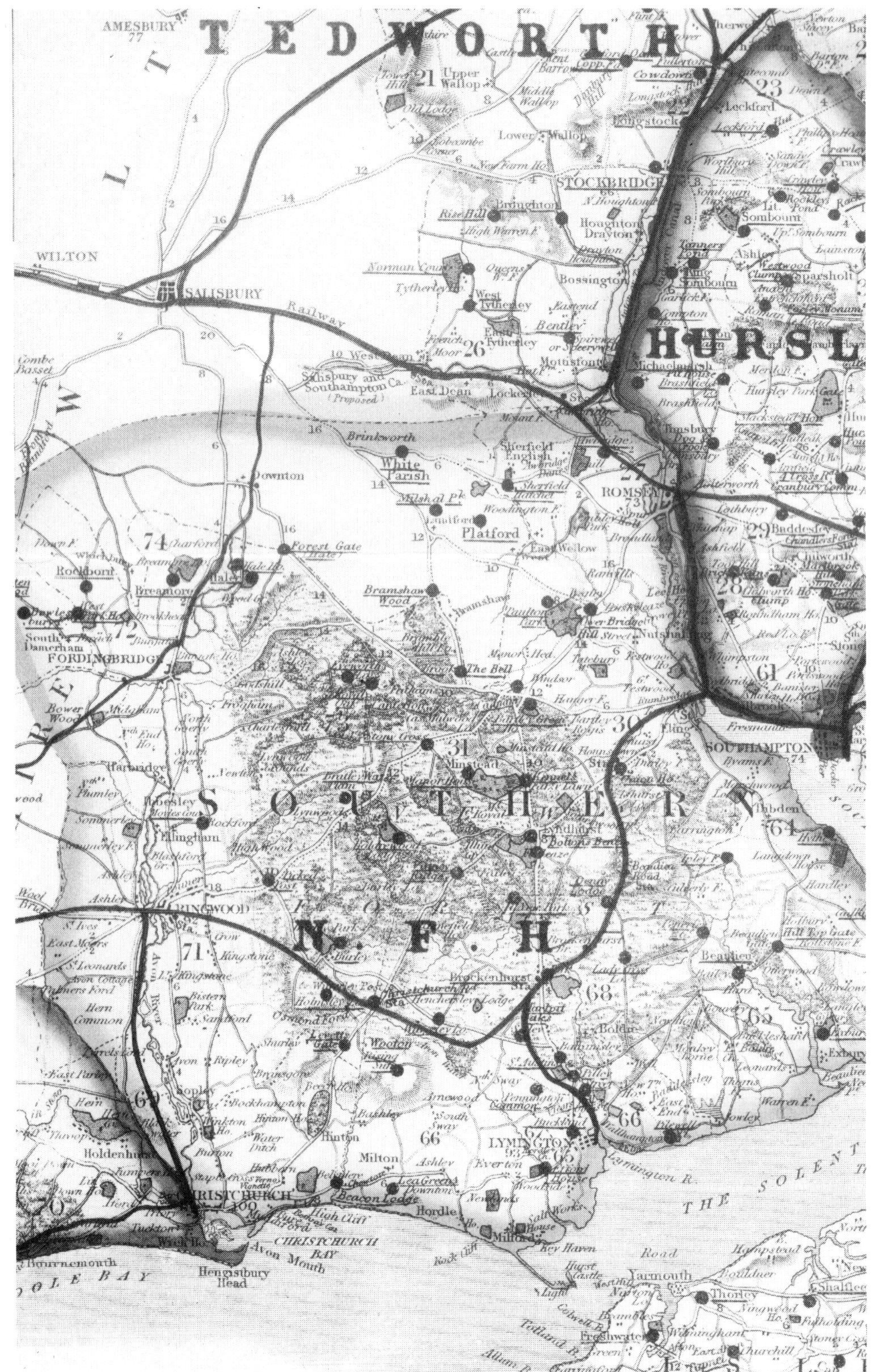

Figure 4.1 The "Country" of the New Forest Hunt

A map of the New Forest during the nineteenth century.

CHAPTER 4

Sam Nicolls

(1814–1828)

Mr Samuel Nicolls succeeded Mr Warde in 1814. His kennel was not large, initially, but he quickly acquired a pack that was cub hunting in October of that year.

YOUTHFUL MASTER

For many years, whilst he was Master of the New Forest Hunt, he was fortunate enough to get a young draft from the Duke of Beaufort's kennels at 'Badminton'. He was a young man of twenty-seven, with a family of two very keen boys, when he took over the Mastership. In spite of his youth, however, he "was a man of quick parts and soon made himself perfect in the science, having taken no small points to become so".[1]

With these good drafts he acquired some fine doghounds and with judicious breeding soon had a pack of some forty couples of hunting hounds. His bitch pack was particularly beautiful and one season they never missed their fox. He had an eye for speed and endurance and was very concerned that the pack should be level. Mr Nicolls used to handle them very quietly and was want to instruct the field in his calm way: "Pray don't halloo gentlemen, for if you once get their heads up I shan't get them down for the rest of the day". In order to ensure the steadiness of his hounds in the Forest he kept a Fallow Deer loose about the kennels.

His Servants

His kennels were at his home, 'Holmfields', opposite Boltons Bench at Lyndhurst, and, breaking with tradition, he hunted hounds himself with Joseph and George Grant as whippers-in, in the early years. Joseph later went on to Lord Kinton and George to Mr Compton at the 'Manor'. They were succeeded by Joe Peckham.

Joe was a rough looking fellow, born in the Forest and "about as hardy as one of its nature oaks". His language to hounds was somewhat unique, as he spoke in monosyllables and a wag once remarked that his high pitched cheer sounded like "a man in an emetic with the dose not quite strong enough for him". However, he was a clever, useful and industrious servant who knew every track in the Forest as well as he knew the back of his own hand.

NEW FOREST JUSTICE — A FAMOUS SIRE

It was during Mr Nicolls' time that the famous hound *New Forest Justice* (1814) was bred[2]. His son, *The Beaufort Justice*, by *New Forest Justice* out of Sir

Thomas Mostyn's *Hopeful*, was the most famous hound of the day; his blood, according to Lord Bathurst, "probably flows in three out of every four foxhounds of the present day", (1925). *New Forest Justice* was used as a stallion hound extensively in the home kennels and also by Sir John Cope. Tradition asserts that he was a "coarse hound, as many, celebrated for their noses, are". He was of immense bone and substance and Mr Nicolls was wont to say he was "as big as a deer".

On his first day out hunting as Master, Mr Nicolls persistently asked the field to resist pressing the hounds and, finally, lost his temper with one offender who expressed his surprise that Mr Nicolls should speak in such an abusive manner to a committee member. To this Mr Nicolls retorted: "The committee be damned! You are not worth damning singly so I'll damn you all in a lump!" He had a very fine voice, a great asset in the Forest, and often, hacking home to the kennels in the dark, he would catch hold of Joe Peckhams whip lash and guide hounds along by cheering and talking to them all the way.

Joe kept a couple of very fine fat pigs of which he was terribly proud. However, on one occasion when Sir John Cope came to stay, he discovered Joe spiriting a sack of hound meal away for his porkers. Mr Nicolls dismissed him but could not manage without him and so took him back again.

The first **Hunt Club Ball** on record was in 1819, at Lyndhurst. The room was appropriately decorated and illuminated and attended by the first in rank and fashion. Even more worthy of note was the fact that they danced the waltz!

The *Sporting Magazine* comments a month later: "English Women cannot waltz without doing violence to some invaluable notions of delicacy and reserve with which they have been brought up".

HUNT CLUB IN 1819

The members of the N.F.H.C. at this time were:

Mr Samuel Nicolls, Lyndhurst.
Mr John Pulteney[3], 'Northerwood House', Lyndhurst.
Mr William Sloane-Stanley, 'Paultons'.
Mr Andrew Berkeley Drummond, 'Cadlands House', Fawley.
Mr Andrew R. Drummond, 'Cadlands House', Fawley.
Mr Henry Combe Compton[4], 'Manor House', Minstead.
Viscount Palmerston, 'Broadlands'.
Mr William Wyndham[5], Dinton, Wiltshire.
Admiral Hyde Parker, Boldre.
Rev. Samuel Heathcote, Bramshaw Hill.
Sir George Rose, 'Cuffnells'.
Mr George Eyre, 'Warrens', Bramshaw.
Lord Cavan, Eaglehurst.
Mr John Morant, 'Brockenhurst House'.
Major E. Gilbert[6], 'Bartley Lodge'.
Mr E. Nightingale, Embley.
Mr H. Timson, Tatchbury.
Sir Charles Hulse, Bart., 'Breamore House'.
Rev. John Lukin[7], Nursling.
Captain Aitcheson R.N., 'Shrubshill', Lyndhurst.
Mr Matthew Monro, 'Fritham Cottage'.
Mr George Harbin, 'Fritham Lodge'.
Mr Charles Phillips, Eling.

Mr R. Bowden-Smith, Lyndhurst.
Lord Montague, 'Beaulieu'.
Lord Hedley,
Lord Lisle[8], 'Moyles Court'.
Mr Chudley Haynes,
Rev. E. Timson[9], Tatchbury.
Rev. W.Wilder, Eling.
Sir Thomas Heathcote, Embley.

HIS PERSONALITY AND APPEARANCE

During the summer months Mr Nicolls was a yachtsman and had a small gaff-rigged cutter named the *Louisa*, which he used to sail in the Solent. On one occasion there was great excitement in the yacht club at a long series of signal flags being flown from the *Louisa*. Code books were consulted but no-one could get the gist of the complicated message. Finally, a boat was sent out to enquire and Mr Nicolls translated: "No. 2 pair of trousers hung up to dry".

His dress was often slipshod, his boots not very well cleaned and his old scarlet coat more plum coloured than anything else. One day they were invited to draw the covert of a newly arrived Forest resident, reputed to be rather particular. Lord Lisle made a point of asking Mr Nicolls to be sure to turn out smartly so as to make a good impression. Mr Nicolls appeared on the day wearing an even older coat than usual, very old boots and breeches and an ancient flat white hat. Joe Peckham wore a stained kennel coat, and had a boot on one leg and a gaiter on the other. The outcome of this flash of humour is not recorded!

Indeed, stories of Mr Nicolls' wit could fill a book by themselves and "Nimrod" quoted many of them in his reports for the popular gentleman's publication of the day *The Sporting Magazine*. Lord Cavan (of "All the Talents" 1803-1808), was on the receiving end when, having drawn the covert at Earldoms blank, hounds were being called out. Lord Cavan rode up to report that he had seen two hounds, *Petticoat* and *Harlot*, running back in cover. "Impossible, my Lord' said the Master "but it tells me what *your* mind is running on!"

NIMROD'S VISITS

The following is the first and longest of "Nimrod's" reports on visits to the Forest in 1825.

"The road from Melton-Mowbray to Lyndhurst, the headquarters of that country, being two miles nearer through my own stableyard than by any other route, my horses refreshed themselves for a few days in their own stalls, and arrived at Lyndhurst on the 10th of April. Taking a peep at London on my road, I mounted the box of the best coach in England (the *Southampton Telegraph*), and on the morning of the same day, working it down the road by the side of those accomplished coachmen, Mr Peere and Mr Taylor, I arrived at Beechwood, the seat of Sir Hussey Vivian, by dinner, and took up my abode under his hospitable roof during my visit to the Forest.

"Although I had never been in "*The* Forest", as it is called, all others being considered quite *infra dig*. to this, yet, having lived a great deal with a friend (Mr Chudleigh Haynes) who took much delight in talking of it, and who but from ill health would never have forsaken it, I fancied myself all but at home.

I had listened with so much pleasure to the many entertaining stories of what had happened there in Mr Warde's, as well as in Mr Nicolls' time (and I believe in no country under the sun, has the "Coffee-house", as it is called, been equal to this), that the names of John Warde, Sam Nicolls, Charles Mitchell, Billy Butler, Jemmy Gilbert, Harbin, Nunez, not forgetting Old Woods and half a score of others, were quite familiar to my ear.

"My readers are aware that the present master of the New Forest Hounds, Mr Nicolls, succeeded the great John Warde, and has now hunted the country nine seasons, with a subscription of about £1,200 per annum. His taste for hounds is allowed to be very correct, and his bitches have been considered about the standard mark.

"The celebrated *New Forest Justice* blood is still going, and nothing can, I believe, excel it. My visit to Sir Hussey extended to the 20th April, during which time I hunted four times with Mr Nicolls; but the same cause (the dry weather) which operated against sport in the country I had just quitted, was in full force there, not a drop of rain having fallen for many weeks. Added to this, there was one other bar, not only to sport, but to all chance of sport, and that was — I am sorry to pronounce it — a lamentable scarcity of foxes. To such an extent, however, I was given to understand, has the unhappy mania for pheasants increased in the precincts of the Forest, that no sooner does a fox stray out of it than he is in a trap. From all I heard, indeed, I have good reason to believe that, were it not for the kindness of his Royal Highness the Duke of York, Head Warden of the Forest, the persons employed under the Lords Commissioners of Woods and Forests, Mr Drummond, the Steward of the Bramber Manor, and a few others well disposed towards foxhunting, there would not be a fox in the country, though the lying for them exceeds anything I ever witnessed before. Brother sportsmen, mind this — *foxhunting trembles on the beam*! and I think I hear hundreds of the rising generation exclaim, 'The sooner it kicks the better, for it is too rough an amusement for us'.

"I saw one very pretty thing with Mr Nicolls pack, running him to ground in twenty-five minutes. The pace was quick enough to show hounds to advantage, and also to show what following them in the New Forest is. The first part was over the open, and latter among the trees and bushes, where the quick running and flying to scent and cry was beautiful to those who could see it. I also saw a great deal of excellent slow-hunting on days in which hounds could have hunted nowhere else: but on all rough ground like the Forest, there is what is called 'a side scent', from the game so often touching with his sides as well as his pads, and which is very favourable to hounds. This description of sport, however, is beautiful to behold, and in some measure suitable to midday hunting in the month of April, when the sun is often hot and oppressive.

"Mr Nicolls hunts his own hounds, assisted by two whippers-in, all very well mounted. Indeed, I do not know when I have seen a more useful stud of hunters than Mr Nicolls'; and Sir Bellingham Graham, who was then staying with him, offered him a large sum for one of them. His weight is a welter, but he rides hard and well across the Forest; and save and except he has to skirt a bog, or is well planted in the middle of it, he is never away from his hounds.

"Mr Nicolls is but a *young master* of foxhounds, and consequently a young huntsman. He is an excellent feeder, and looks to essential points, in shape and make. He is not like some masters of hounds that I could name, all for legs and feet, nearly regardless of other form, but has an eye to points for speed and lasting. His style of hound struck me as being particularly good, and I might also add, that when we have seen a few of his kennel, we have seen them all. Mr Nicolls looks like a true-born Englishman who is not ashamed of his country — which is more than we can say of all we meet.

"He is not a dandy, we must admit, but he has cultivated his mind more than his dress; and, amongst other accomplishments, Mr Nicolls is a poet of a very pretty turn. As a master of foxhounds, however, I saw nothing in the least magisterial or imperious in Mr Nicolls in the field; on the contrary, he was polite and obliging to all. As a companion, Mr Nicolls is a man of great readiness of wit, and a happy quickness in reply. A well-mounted man had one day been pressing so closely on his hounds that nothing but a Job could stand it any longer, and Mr Nicolls bestowed upon him a few hearty damns. The offender rode up to him, and said, 'Upon my word Mr Nicolls, I don't understand this, sir. I did not *come out* to be damned.' 'Then *go home* and be damned!', replied Mr Nicolls.[10]

"It being the Easter holidays, I had the pleasure of seeing one part of Mr Nicolls' establishment which I should otherwise have missed, and that was his two sons in the field. The eldest (my friend Sam, about twelve years of age) will rate and turn a hound with any man in England; and as for the youngest (only seven years old), in his scarlet coat and hunting-whip, he and his pony are allowed to be quite unique. This is training up a child in the way *he should go*, and it will take a good horseman to go better than my friend Sam Nicolls, jun., over the forest.[11]

"The New Forest is a very awkward country to get across, and one in which, in my opinion, there is no great enjoyment of hounds, when they go the pace. Fences are generally to be managed, but bogs require wings; and as heart of oak is rather harder than men's skulls, another difficulty presents itself in the wooded parts — a tree is to be encountered at about every fourth stride of the horse. Horses that are used to all this soon become wonderfully handy; but, taking it all together, the Forest is a distressing country to them, although they get a few chances in their favour by foxes running short, which, from the nature of the country they must often do.

"There was one person in the Forest of whom, having heard so much, I was particularly anxious to see, and that was Mr Harbin.[12]

"This gentleman resides in the Forest, and, like the oaks that overshadow it, he has not been stinted in his growth. His weight on his horse must be upwards of twenty stone, but his seat on his saddle surprised me much. He stood up in his stirrups, in his thin jockey boots, as his horse galloped along, and displayed all the activity of a ten stone man. He is also allowed to be an excellent sportsman, and knows every track. I have singular circumstance to relate of Mr Harbin, which I heard from his own mouth.

"On my speaking to him in praise of his chestnut horse, for a finer animal eyes never beheld, he told me that it was glandered for four seasons, but it made no difference in his work, and he is now quite well.

"Lyndhurst still remains the capital of the Forest, and several gentlemen (among whom were those celebrated sportsmen, Mr Templer, Mr Spurrier,

Figure 4.2 "Slodens"

A well-kept ride — typical New Forest scene in a forestry enclosure.

(*Photo courtesy:* John A. Belcher)

and Mr J. Codrington) were staying at *The Crown*. Sir Bellingham Graham was on a visit to Mr Nicolls; Mr John Moore was staying with Mr Compton; and Sir John Cope and Mr Warde were also to have been with Mr Nicolls, but were prevented by slight indisposition.

"Sir Hussey Vivian's father was on a visit to him when I was in the Forest, and is an example to all men of the good effects of a country life and country sports. Mr Vivian resides at Trewan, in Cornwall, where he has kept hounds for a great number of years (hunting fox after Christmas) and where he fulfils some of the most important offices of a country gentleman. Although nearly arrived at the 'age of man', Mr Vivian is young in condition, and as firm and strong a horseman as I ever met with.

"On the second day of my hunting with Mr Nicolls, I had the pleasure of seeing 'Billy Butler'; the well known Mr Butler. Although we had never met we had heard and read of each other, and slight introduction put us completely at our ease.

"Mr Butler informed me that the last was the *fortieth month of April* in succession that he had spent in the Forest, but gave it as his opinion that, should he live to see forty years more, foxhunting in the Forest would only be talked of *as having once been*.

"When his Majesty — then the Prince of Wales — hunted in Dorsetshire, where Mr Butler resides, he was extremely pleased with his society, and bestowed upon him several slight marks of his attention, and which I understand he continues to do to this day.

"Every one, indeed, must be pleased with Mr Butler. There is about him a simplicity of manner, added to a quaintness of expression, very rarely met with in these sophisticated days, to which an additional zest is given by a powerful Dorsetshire dialect. As a sportsman, a companion, and a worthy, excellent man, however, Mr Butler ranks with any one, and his name is as well known in the Western hemisphere of the sporting world as Russell's waggons are on the Western road. As may be expected, the gentleman I have been speaking of — being quite an original — does not only afford amusement to his friends, but is now and then himself the subject of a harmless joke. On the last day of my visit to Sir Hussey, he had a large party to dinner, amongst whom was Mr Butler, and by accident he was placed opposite an excellent painting of a fox by Barenger. It so happened that Mr Butler never saw this fox till he had taken his glass of port wine after his cheese, when he suddenly exclaimed, 'What a beautiful picture of a fox!', 'Ah, Billy', said an old friend of his, who sat opposite to him, 'how well your nose must have been down this last hour, that you never saw that fox before!' Sir Hussey lives well."

"Nimrod"

TRAGEDY

In late 1827, a domestic tragedy occurred. Mrs Nicolls was terribly injured in a carriage accident and was close to death. Mr Nicolls was grief stricken and felt unable to hunt hounds. He therefore asked Colonel John Cooke, of Droxford, to stand in for him. This well known old sportsman was, in fact, dying of cancer of the tongue at the time, but hunted the pack till the end of the season. His book, *Observations on Foxhunting*, is well worth reading, for the flavour of the times floats out of every page and, as he was a local man, born at Christchurch and brought up at 'Cuffnells' whilst he was still an infant by Sir George Rose after his parents death, he speaks of the Forest fondly and with first hand knowledge.

In 1828 Mr Nicolls resigned, selling his pack to Lord Kintore of **The Vale of White Horse**, for 1,000 guineas. On his last day as Master he could not let the occasion pass without one final witticism. Apparently he had not been seeing eye-to-eye with all members and supporters since he had given his resignation and was somewhat hurt by their attitude. His field, as usual, were pressing and one hound *Gratitude* was overridden. "For Gods sake, don't kill Gratitude" quoth the Master, "it is already reduced to a hounds name."

In addition to all his other abilities, Mr Nicolls was an accomplished poet, (see end of Chapter 3, page 34). For many years after he had taken over the New Forest Hunt he used to correspond with Mr John Warde at the **Craven**, in verse. Mr Stephen Terry, the renowned diarist refers to him often in his journals and sums him up as "very clever, given to jocularity, his ardour and language in a burst run, most animating".[13] He was killed in the field in the early 1850s, whilst out hunting with the Pytcheley, near Misterton.

HUNTING DIARY 1814-1828

October 1825

"**The Bramshaw Day**. Hounds ran by Paultons, through Embley and onto Broadlands. At Embley, Sir Thomas Heathcote had left instructions that coverts were not to be disturbed as there was to be a shooting party on the morrow. At Broadlands the gates were locked and neither hounds nor field could find a place in the stout wall which they could get over. Finally in desperation Mr Nicolls ordered Joe Peckham to dismount and burst the gate open so that at least hounds could get in, remarking 'This is foxhunting with a vengence. First we are prohibited by a Baronet and then locked out by a Lord'. Lord Palmerston obviously found the whole thing very amusing, and sent down to the gate, that the master and field were invited to join him for lunch."

Taken from *The Sporting Magazine*, by "Nimrod".

Brockenhurst Day

"**Brockenhurst Day**. From Brockenhurst hounds ran across New Park and Mr Nicolls called out to Sir Bellingham Graham, that there was a deer fence (4 foot high palings and double ditch) in front of them so that they must find a gate. Sir Bellingham, a celebrated foxhunter from the Shires (and subsequently to become MFH of the Hambledon for a short time) ignored the warning and rode on with Mr Tom Smith in his wake. Sir Bellingham's horse *Beeswax* managed the fence and ditch but pecked on landing whilst Tom Smiths *The General* cleared the lot perfectly. Sir Bellingham promptly offered 250 guineas for *The General* which was, equally promptly, refused, although he was a newly acquired asset at only 45 guineas. At a later date hunting in the Shires he was offered even larger sums which were also turned down."

Taken from *Annals of Sport*.

NOTES

1 *The Sporting Magazine*, 1825, page 393.

2 *Justice* was bred by Mr Wyndham of Dinton, Wiltshire; the father of the subsequent Master.

3 Mr John Pulteney was one of the chief supporters of Mr Nicolls. In addition to never missing a day's sport, he donated some 300 guineas a year, towards the upkeep of hounds.

4 Mr Henry Combe Compton also had a house in Quorndon and hunted there frequently; when at Eton he and George Osbaldeston walked to Ascot and back to see one race between school hours. Although he was three years younger than 'Squire' Osbaldeston the friendship lasted throughout their adult lives.

5 Mr William Wyndham was the subsequent Master — see next chapter.

6 **Major Edward Gilbert**. Known widely as 'Jemmy', the nickname given to him as a child by his father, Vincent Hawkins Gilbert, founder of the Hunt. Major Gilbert was reported as a bold rider and a "famous performer", visiting many hunts locally, and around Melton. He was a man good at everything and was once very badly injured by a fall with the **Quorn** hounds whilst staying with Mr Compton. He was one of a *very few* who saw the end of one of the most severe runs Osbaldeston ever had in the **Quorn** country. The distance from point to point was 18 miles but hounds ran hard for two hours and seventeen minutes, so that much more ground must have been covered.

7 **Rev. John Lukin**. A celebrated Forest character from Nursling. "No greater sportsman ever bestrode a pigskin." He was a very pretty rider, a lightweight, and rode a flighty grey whose ambition in life was to unship his rider. The Reverend gentleman used to wind the horse's mane around his hands and quietly sit out the display. One day the rider in front of him came off on a fast run and was floundering around in the bottom of a deep drainage ditch. "Lie still, lie still, Sir" called out Mr Lukin "and let the old parson ride over you". He was renowned as being something of a dandy, always wearing yellow leather breeches.

8 **Lord Lisle, of Millbrook**. He had a "wonderful broken knee'd cob" — a very hard rider.

9 **Rev. E. Timson**. Subsequently Master N.F.H. 1845–60.

10 The offender was a regular subscriber; Mr Alison a barber from Southampton. He used to hunt on an old grey mare and also hunted with the **Hambledon**.

11 **Sam Nicolls**. Subsequently became Master of the **Hursley** 1869-1888. His twenty years of good management marked a golden era in the **Hursley's** history. When he took over the management the hunt was in poor case with a total subscription of only £300 a year. He very quickly improved matters and the subscription (guarantee) rose to £1,000.

12 Mr Harbin died aged seventy-six at Fritham on 3rd May, 1837. *The Sporting Magazine* printed a memoir for this popular character. A fine compliment as this was normally reserved for the Melton celebrities. He is reported riding "A la Chiffney standing up in his stirrups having his horse fast by the head in a plain snaffle and going a slapping pace". He was certainly among the founder members of the Hunt and Mr Gilbert refers to him in his diary as "my good friend and chief supporter from Fritham".

13 The Drummer Diaries.

14 Zach Goddard.

Figure 4.3 Hunting Dress

Showing the attire worn for hunting, c. 1820.

5

The Great Western

1828–1854

Figure 5.1 A Hunting Scene

(Taken from an old print)

CHAPTER 5

The Great Western

1828–1854

MR WYNDHAM

Upon Mr Nicolls' resignation in 1828, Mr William Wyndham came from Wiltshire and took on the Mastership. He was of a somewhat serious turn of mind in contrast to both the previous Masters, whose amusing witticisms had kept the pens of visiting sporting journalists busy.

One of his first acts was to move the kennels from Lyndhurst to 'Burntford House' at Bramshaw and, in the early years, William Butler and Henry Gillet turned hounds to him.

The removal of the kennels caused much regret, as the correspondent "Nimsouth" (none other than the famous "**Surtees**", who was, at a later date, the author of the *Jorrocks* series), wrote: "The removal of the kennel to Bramshaw, five miles from Lyndhurst is certainly a disadvantage, for on a pouring wet day what is an unfortunate individual to do with himself? There are few sportsmen who cannot pass an hour or two in a kennel very agreeably. It used to be a great lounge during Mr Nicolls' time, who from all accounts must have been very admirable in the Forest; indeed, his humour alone was worth any money".

Mr Wyndham came from a well known hunting family, his father having kept a "very smart" pack at Dinton, Wiltshire, with which he hunted over the **South and West Wilts**, and the **Wilton** countries. His brother-in-law, Charles Codrington, had been Master of the **Old Berkshire Hunt** and subsequently founded the **South Wilts Hunt** in 1824 or thereabouts.

The new Master had learned much from these useful contacts and although his hounds tended to be slower and more lumbering than their predecessors in the Forest, he was soon showing good sport as hounds were capital line-hunters.

Shortly after he took over the New Forest, he became engaged to Ellen, the daughter of a neighbour — the Reverend Samuel Heathcote of Bramshaw Hill. The marriage took place in 1831 and was of course, "well attended by foxhunters from far and near". The bride was the grand-daughter of Sir Thomas Heathcote, a founder member of the New Forest Hunt Club.

In November 1834, whilst hunting near Burley, a very sad thing happened. Lord Lisle, an ardent supporter of the New Forest Hunt and a dedicated lifelong foxhunter, fell from his horse in a fit. He died almost instantly.

In 1835 there is a record of two new hunt servants, Sam Powell, and Sharp who had previously been at the **Hambledon**.

VISIT OF THE ROYAL BUCKHOUNDS

The **Royal Buckhounds** visited the Forest in April 1836, the first meet being at Boltons Bench, Lyndhurst. Over 2,000 people were at the first meet and many distinguished sportsmen had turned out to have a day with the distinguished pack under the management of the Earl of Errol, including no less than fourteen visiting M.F.H.s.

In one of his many illuminating articles, "Nimrod" wrote at this time on the New Forest:

"The lying is so strong with gorse and blackthorn that after a certain hour in the day, hounds do not care to go far into them, unless accompanied by their huntsman and this is difficult because of the blind drains with which they abound.

"In case of a fox slipping away it is dangerous for a huntsman to accompany them dismounted, as he may never catch his hounds! On the other hand if he holloas them in from the rides, half of them will not obey the holloa, but remain at the horses heels. What then is to be done?

"Why, a whipper-in is sent into the Coverts *on foot* encouraging the hounds, to draw them, and this succeeds well. The plan originated with Mr Nicolls . . ."

The Hon. Grantley Berkeley, in his book, *Reminiscences of a Huntsman* records: "The oddest system that I ever saw with hounds was William Wyndham, and he occasionally broached opinions that I could not reconcile with anything I had learned by former experience. His plan seemed to me, to be, to do nothing, and I have been told that he has said, that when a hound distinguished himself in the pack by making a wonderful hit, he always drafted him, it being wrong in his opinion, that one hound should distinguish himself from the others . . . Still I saw enough of his system to feel quite sure that his foxes had a jubilee, and that unless there was such a scent as forced the hounds to come along, neither Mr Wyndham's exertions nor that of his hounds would make a bad day middling, nor a middling one satisfactory".

It should be stated here that Mr Berkeley and Mr Wyndham had an extreme dislike of each other. On one occasion Mr Wyndham had complained by letter to Mr Berkeley, that because of an action of his, Mrs Wyndham had suffered the loss of her peace of mind. In Mr Berkeley's reply is the terse rejoinder: "As to your charge for the loss of Mrs Wyndham's peace of mind on this occasion, that is absurd; considering the time you have been married, she could not have any to lose".

It is clear, however, from reports in *The Sporting Magazine* that the standard of hunting declined somewhat during the latter years of Mr Wyndham's mastership and there was a certain amount of dissatisfaction among the Hunt Club members.

One of the popular characters of the Forest at this time was Mr Richard 'Dicky' Wyse. He was the driver of the Southampton to Alresford coach, the old "*Southampton Union*", and, depending upon where he happened to be on the day, he hunted with either the **H.H.** or the **New Forest.** On one occasion he had arranged to exchange horses with Mr Jack Hewitt, a Southampton butcher, who "used to horse a couple of coaches". As it turned out neither man had ever seen the other's horse, until the day came to do the swop. Wyse's horse was a roarer, and Hewitt's was spavined. Hewitt, discovering on the first day the quality of his new acquisition decided to say nothing. On the second day, however, Mr Wyse passed his shop hacking home from hunting "on three legs", and called out "No friendship in horse-dealing, Mr Hewitt, no friendship in horse-dealing". Another day a parson who was so unfortunate as to be "bald, knock-kneed and very plain of feature", said to Mr Wyse, "That is a very ugly horse you are on", "Yes sir", replied Dicky, "and I should say that beauty was not by when you was dropped either!".[1]

HIS COUSIN — THE GREAT WESTERN

In 1838 Mr Wyndham resigned from the Forest as he felt he should spend more time at Dinton where his father was in failing health. He then hunted the **South Wilts** country at his own expense for ten years, having succeeded to the family estates in 1841.

He handed the house at Bramshaw, including the kennels and some hounds, to his brother-in-law, Mr Charles William Codrington, known nationally as **The Great Western**. The nickname becomes self-explanatory when we learn that he rode at 22 stone. He did not hunt hounds himself, engaging George Whitmere as huntsman and Edwards, known as "Humpy David", as whipper-in.

Mr Codrington was a thorough sportsman and "very gentlemanly in the field". He was considered by his brother foxhunters to be "a perfect oracle on everything appertaining to the Noble Science. Mr Codrington's recollection of pedigrees of foxhounds were marvellous and his knowledge as huntsman in the field was quite perfection, although his great weight prevented him from keeping a very forward place".

In 1814 he had married the eldest daughter of Mr Wyndham at Dinton (the previous Master's elder sister), and had since then, prior to coming to the Forest, been Master of three packs.

His hounds were somewhat racier than the previous pack. He took over the Mastership in October 1838 and only one month later the weekly newspaper *Bell's Life* records "good fun in the Forest". "On 20th November, the N.F.H. met at Rhinefield; found near Lyndhurst and ran very fast through the New Park Enclosures. Then away from the open, leaving most of the field inside, as fast as hounds could run up to Heathy Ditton, and killed as he was crawling over a bank. This was a very quick thing. Mr John Drummond in long black boots, riding a magnificent grey horse went well with hounds as did Major Gilbert and Mr Timson." The Hon. Grantley Berkeley speaks warmly of Mr Codrington: "No man knew more of hunting than he did, or how he should, or would have done it, had he been anything within riding weight. People called him slow, and he could not, in his person, well be otherwise; but Mr Codrington made his system suit his personal capabilities for, if hounds ran hard, he saw none of the fun. If he had men out with him to whom he wished to show a run, he used to say to hounds, as they went into cover: 'There, go and find your fox, and when you have found him, I hope I shan't see you again for two hours. Then you'll have had a good run, and killed him'. Before I was used to Mr Codringtons way of talking to himself we ran a fox in the Great Ridge, and suddenly went away over the open with a scent. Hounds ran hard for fifteen minutes and then, inexplicably, threw up. They did not know me, and there was no-one 'to put 'em along', if I had known what to do. But so sudden was the check with nothing that I could see to cause it, that had they been my own hounds, I should scarcely have known what remedy to apply. I sat looking on, with some suspicion of riot, when, a long way off down wind, I heard the most painful groans, mingled with deprecations. My first idea was that it came from a delirious suffering fellow creature, being dragged perhaps, in his stirrup. I could not see the person who seemed in such mortal agony, for the contours of the ground, but presently I heard the hollow sounds of a horses feet, and up over the rise came Mr Codrington, all right, but moaning dreadfully. I set off to meet him, anxiously enquiring 'What was the matter?'. 'Matter?, Oh Lord!' he cried, 'Come up horse!' and then rolling in his saddle he cried, 'Matter?, Oh Lord, its nothing but a hare'.

"He called the hounds and we returned to our woodland fox. Afterwards, at Wilverly, observing that he was riding a queer looking animal for such a weight, I asked 'What is that you are on?'. 'Oh Lord!' he cried, 'All I know is that it is not a hunter'."

Mr Stephen Terry, of Dummer, wrote of Mr Codrington, ". . . he is a very agreeable man, called the Great Western, about 22 stone. Horses always seem uncomfortable under him, he constantly chides them. He sold six couple of hounds for £600, a great price at that time, though not now".

METHOD OF HUNTING

He adopted the old system of leaving hounds to find the fox themselves, by trusting them to draw wide, and carried out this system of drawing so that people were surprised to see how long he would remain in one spot whilst his hounds spread out far and wide around him. According to Major Gilbert, the son of the founder, Mr Codrington's pack were by far the most unsizeable he had ever seen. It was very mixed and contained specimens of the largest and smallest possible foxhounds. So long as they ran and worked well together, and on this point he was most particular, he did not object to any disparity in size or conformation.

He was well known for his habit of talking to himself out hunting and for constantly nudging and chiding his horses, "Whey . . .! Come up there horse!", when it was not even stirring an ear.

In August 1842 he died suddenly, much regretted by his many friends in the Forest and in the foxhunting world, generally. His hounds went to Mr W. Wyndham's younger brother Francis.

PROBLEMS OF CONTINUITY

The vacant country was immediately advertised but being so late in the season not one reply was received. It looked very much as though there would be a blank year.

Andrew Drummond met Major Edward Gilbert at the next meeting of the Hunt Club and they discussed this outrageous state of affairs. Mr Gilbert said that if the hounds and money could be found he would undertake to hunt hounds himself — rather than let the Forest go unhunted.

Mr Drummond went home and thought about this and a week later wrote to Mr Gilbert asking him what would be the cost of hunting a scratch pack of fifteen couples for the following winter.

His reply was by return; "I am surprised that no-one more influential cannot be found. However, I will do it for £650, to include 'cloathes', keep of hounds, huntsmen, whipper-in and feeder; then nothing left for earth-stopping, and that cost Mr Codrington last season £140".

Nothing evidently came of this for the next record is of a meeting at Stoney Cross, probably at the 'Compton Arms Hotel', on 10th October, 1842 where it was unanimously resolved "that the proposal of Mr Lindsay Shedden to hunt the Forest on five days a fortnight for £500, keeping a huntsman and whipper-in, should be accepted. Also that the Hunt Club members would afford every support in their power to assist Mr Shedden and that one half of the sum subscribed by any member should be paid into Messrs. Madisons Banks at Southampton on or before 1st November next, and the remainder on or before 1st March, 1843.

CAPTAIN LINDSAY SHEDDON

Therefore, Mr, or rather Captain, Sheddon, for he had formerly been an officer with the 17th Lancers, became the new Master. At the time of his appointment there were no hounds, no horses and no kennels. He was living, at the time, in Lymington so there was no question of housing hounds there.

Nevertheless, he boldly advertised the opening meet for four weeks hence, on the 15th November at Boltons Bench, Lyndhurst, and set about arranging matters. The first thing he did was to hastily errect some temporary buildings at 'Woodlands'; and these were filled just as quickly. Horses were bought and a pack of hounds — they were mainly drafts from the **Quorn**. These hounds were not broken to deer and the fact that there were some 5,000 Fallow Deer in the Forest at that time gave some initial headaches. Joe Peckham "as hard as one of the Forest oaks", who had been at the **Hambledon** since Mr Nicolls' resignation, came to the Forest to hunt hounds for Captain Sheddon in that first difficult year.

A CAPITAL HUNT

By the end of the first season he was showing excellent sport and in April 1843 there were several reports of "Spring Hunting in the New Forest" in the popular journals. Towards the end of April Mr Wyndham had a few days with the N.F.H. as he wished to see his old country hunted, and the new hounds. It so happened that the bitch pack was out twice, on two of his planned three days hunting. The scent was very good and they consequently had a great deal of rushing about, but little steady hunting. Mr Wyndham remarked that he should like to have seen more of the dog pack, whereupon Captain Sheddon replied that if Mr Wyndham would stay another day he would oblige as, "there was an outlying fox in a covert near Ringwood; we will try to find him and see if we can have some hunting".

He was found; went straight away fast and was run into in the open at 'Woodlands', near Ashurst at the other end of the country. A 12 mile fast point lasting sixty-five minutes. Very few were up at the finish, as may perhaps, be expected considering the country they traversed. Mr Wyndham told Captain Sheddon that it was the finest hunt he had ever seen.

There is another record of that season's spring hunting, when the **Royal Staghounds** visited and met at Stoney Cross with Lord Rosslyn as Master.

That first difficult season over, the Captain and the leading members, particularly Andrew R. Drummond, John Pulteney and Mr Sloane-Stanley (the latter was the Chairman at that time), set about arranging things in a more formal manner.

THE KENNELS

The first, and main problem was the lack of proper kennels. A meeting was held at 'The Crown', Lyndhurst, in April 1843 to decide what was to be done. With characteristic generosity 'Harry' Compton gave a piece of land at 'Furzey Lawn', just a mile out of Lyndhurst. The understanding at this meeting appears to have been that if, for six years in succession, no hounds should be kept there, then the land should revert to the Compton estate.

The minute of that meeting reads:

"It is proposed that a kennel and stable be built in an eligible situation to belong to the New Forest Hunt Club, the same to be vested in trustees, by a deed specifying the purpose for which they hold them. It is supposed that £1,000 will be required to effect these objects which it is proposed to raise by issuing shares of £50 each — the principal proprieters in the Forest to be offered the same."

Mr John Pulteney of 'Northerwood' had the buildings designed and actually financed the whole whilst the money was being raised. He was to have been paid 3% on this expenditure but in the event he never was paid this interest. He also housed the hounds during the period that the building was taking place.

On the 18th October, 1843, he wrote to Andrew Drummond: "The solidity of structure, and increase in accommodation, has augmented the outlay of the kennel establishment, and I must appeal to your generosity and that of my fellow subscribers for an additional enrollment of shares to meet the occasion. The work is of the best and comprises an accommodation for fifty couples of hounds, and more. Stabling for ten horses, and house room for the requisite number of hunting servants".

In the event the cost was £1,740. The shares were issued as follows:

Lord Palmerston	2 shares	£100
Sir C. Hulse	2 shares	£100
Mr John Pulteney	4 shares	£200
Mr Sloane-Stanley	2 shares	£100
Mr H. Compton	2 shares	£100
Capt. Robbins (Hon. Sec)	2 shares	£100
Capt. Shedden	5 shares	£250
Mr Mills	1 share	£50
Mr Eyre	2 shares	£100
Mr A. Drummond	4 shares	£200
Col. Buckley	1 share	£50
Mr Chamberlayne	1 share	£50
Sir F. Bathurst	1 share	£50
Anonymous	1 share	£50

Figure 5.2 The Kennels

The kennels of the New Forest Hounds and the kennel-huntsman's cottage. The land was donated by Henry Coombe Compton in 1843 and the buildings paid for by subscription of the Club members.

(*Photo courtesy:* John A. Belcher)

The balance appears to have been met by Mr Pulteney. They next turned to the hounds. Captain Sheddon had already arranged to take the entire **Hursley** pack from April and Mr Thomas Ashetton-Smith kindly provided him with a draft of twelve to fifteen couples that year and for the few years following. It was very difficult at that time to get walkers for puppies and consequently few were bred. In time, therefore, the pack consisted, almost entirely, of Mr Thomas Ashetton-Smith's breed.

Henry Gillet came in as huntsman, and was the first occupant of the cottage at 'Furzey Lawn' which, today, still houses the principal hunt servant. He stayed three seasons and was replaced by William Chapelow.

LADY RIDERS AND OTHER MATTERS

Mrs Marjorie Sheddon was a beautiful horsewoman and hunted every day. Although there is a brief mention of ladies hunting occasionally before this date, it seems to be in 1843 that they hunted in any numbers in the Forest. Lady Rose Lovell, Mrs Robbins, Mrs Rowley, and Miss Gore (afterwards Lady Edward Thynne) were all noted by *The Sporting Magazine* as going well.

At this time the Hunt also formed a cricket team. The chief stars being Francis Compton (who also played for Hampshire), Paulet Compton, H. Morant and T. Onslow; Arnold of Cambridge was their professional bowler. In the summer months they played against teams from adjacent packs as well as local teams on the old cricket ground at Lyndhurst.

In to this cloudless period came the **railway**! Everyone foretold the end to hunting. In 1846 Hans Sloane-Stanley wrote a note to Andrew Drummond, "I hear from George (Robbins) that hounds are to be given up after this season. The railroads will ruin the country entirely".

In the event of course, Captain Shedden did not give up hounds, and hunting went on quite tranquilly until 1851. In spring of that year disaster struck! Every hound in the kennels was lost with distemper. The Master resigned and it seemed for a while that this really was the end of hunting in the Forest.

Andrew Robert Drummond, Esquire, of 'Cadlands', was most upset about this, and was indefatigable in his efforts to get things started again. He wrote to all the important personages in the area. To Lord Palmerston: "I think it is a shame and a disgrace that the New Forest is to be without a pack of Foxhounds". Lord Palmerston entirely agreed and offered his assurances that he would continue to subscribe if Mr Drummond was able to re-establish a pack. To 'Harry' Compton: ". . . a disgrace for this country that has been hunted for so long not to have hounds . . .", and so on. All the replies were affirmative. But what was to be done?

RE-ESTABLISHMENT

Lindsay Sheddon was asked to take on a re-established pack, if one could be got together. He agreed, provided a guarantee of £650 could be made, and provided he could get the hounds.

The next months were spent frantically writing to M.F.H.'s all over the kingdom begging for the odd couple. They were fortunate and eventually got together thirty-two couples from the **Pytcheley**, Lord Fitzharding, the

Atherstone and **Lowndes.** Mr Francis Lovell wrote to his father-in-law, the Duke of Beaufort, and persuaded him to part with a couple. Thomas Ashetton-Smith regretted that he could not help until the following spring but enclosed a generous cheque which was to be used to "bribe a suitable Master". Ashetton-Smith had been a constant visitor to the Forest for many years and agreed heartily that foxhunting there "must go on".

Hunting started again in mid-November, and for the next two years Captain Sheddon, now living at 'Elcombes', in Lyndhurst hunted hounds himself. He gave up in 1853 however, being unable to support the financial burden of the Mastership any longer.

During the entire period of Lindsay Sheddon's Mastership, sport was exceptional and points of 10 and 12 miles made regular reports in the sporting press. Of course there were not at that time, the enclosures, which later were to cover the Forest and cause foxes to "run shorter".

He was a popular man, entertaining often and, together with his lovely wife, was unsparing in his efforts to improve Forest hunting, increase the numbers of local sportsmen who supported hounds and to encourage the members of the Hunt Club to play a more active role in 'managing' the country.

No fewer than forty-three new members were elected to the Hunt Club during his eleven years of office so that when he relinquished the reins in 1853, everything was in good heart.

His last day as Master saw a magnificent hunt from Brockenhurst. The immense field of happy supporters came up after the fox was accounted for, to thank him and congratulate him on the day's sport. As usual he was first up with hounds at the end — in spite of the fact that he rode at 16 stone at the time.

Mr Theobald

The country was advertised in good time, and the most suitable candidate was Mr Theobald Theobald who had previously hunted the **Devon & Somerset Staghounds** and latterly the country between Bath and Warminster. At a meeting at 'The Compton Arms' at Stoney Cross in April he agreed to hunt the country three days a fortnight, with a Bye* whenever possible, for £650, there being promises by local landowners to take care of earth-stopping on their respective properties.

Accordingly, Mr Theobald moved to Lyndhurst, taking on the lease of 'Forest Lodge', a convenient short walk from the kennel establishment. He recruited Smith, who was formerly with Lord Fokestone's harriers, as his huntsman, and Frank Walker and Will Chapelow (the son of Mr Shedden's huntsman), turned hounds to him.

His Mastership was uneventful and lasted only one season, the country not being to his liking. He found great difficulty in keeping hounds sound and complained bitterly about the "New Forest Lameness". This odd phenomena had been well known for years and it was well written about. Some blamed furzey plants, others blamed the mud. Certainly it was being discussed in 1804 and still being written about in 1910.

*An extra, unscheduled hunting day.

Figure 5.3 Earth Stopping — an indispensable part of fox-hunting.

(Taken from an old print c. 1831.)

There are few accounts of hunting days during Mr Theobald's time and in 1854, having given his resignation, he returned to his home in Sutton Courteney, near Abingdon, subsequently becoming Master of the **Craven** from 1858-1862.

In 1853, owing to ill-health, Hans Sloane-Stanley had resigned his position as Chairman. He said he was ". . . suffering from an incurable disease that it seems I shall never be able to throw my leg over a horse again". Mr Andrew Robert Drummond was, therefore, invited to take this office which, staunch supporter as he was, he was pleased to accept.

HUNTING DIARY 1828-1854

November 1839

"A fox found at No Man's Land near Bramshaw was hunted by these hounds for three hours and taken at Grimstead near Salisbury. 'Humpy David' was the only one with them at the end, and he had to ask their line several times as they ran so fast. This was a point of 12 miles and probably double that as hounds ran."

28th December, 1839

"After a meet at Wilverly Post hounds found in Homsley Enclosure, and the fox took them over Picket Post Plain round the outside of Roe, through Milkham, across Broomy Plain, through Broomy, through Sloden and Amberwood to Ashley. However, here in the open he was headed and hounds ran into him after a capital hunt of 1 hour and 50 minutes. Of a field of 60 horsemen only four besides the hunt staff were up at the end. They were Mr Henry Coombe Compton, L.B. Mackinnon and Colonel Robbins."

9th December, 1843

"Captain Lindsay Shedden's hounds met at Vinney Ridge and found in Holm Hill a fine fox who went over Feltham Flats, via the Eagles Nest (Eagle Oak?) to Bratley Plain. He was run into on the banks of Bratley Water after fifty-five minutes racing. Amongst those up were the Master, Colonel Robbins, Mr Compton, M.P., Mr H. Compton, Mr Buckworth Powell, Mr Carnac, Sir Henry Paulet, Mr Martin Powell and Mr Mackinnon."

The above extracts were taken from *The Sporting Review*.

April 1850

"The New Forest Hounds had a series of excellent runs on the 8th from Beaulieu, when Col. Lawrenson, Colonel Parker, Mr Mills, General Robbins and Captain Sheddon had the best of it, and on the 11th, Bramshaw, whence they had a fine run of one hour and a quarter; and first this day were Mr E. Timson and Captain Powell."

Taken from *Sporting Reminiscences of Hampshire*, by "Aesop".

NOTES

1 J.F.R. Hope in *Hunting in Hampshire*, 1950.
2 The Diaries of Dummer.
3 Most of the excerpts from letters in this chapter are from records kept at 'Cadlands House', Fawley.

6

Messrs. Timson, Morant and Standish

1854–1874

Figure 6.1 A Hunting Centre — The New Forest

(Taken from an old print)

CHAPTER 6

Messrs. Timson, Morant and Standish

1854–1874

Having accepted Mr Theobald's resignation in the spring of 1854, the committee met at 'The Crown', Lyndhurst, to decide on the future hunting of the country. It was proposed by Mr Francis Lovell that a suitable advertisement be placed in *Bell's Life*. This was agreed and the following rather quaint advertisement duly appeared.

"To the great regret of the gentlemen of the country, the Mastership of The New Forest Hounds has become vacant. We hope that this fine country with such an adequate subscription will not be long without a Master . . ."

A subsequent meeting was adjourned when the committee was unable to reach agreement on the suitability of any of the applicants.

At this juncture a member, the Rev. Edward Timson, of 'Tatchbury Mount', Calmore, came forward with an offer to run the country three times a week with a subscription of £750. It appears that he was accepted with some relief, for the gentlemen present at the meeting immediately drew up a list and guaranteed the sum required between them.

Mr Timson at once set about buying a pack of hounds. Based on his opinion that it would take a pack from a rough country to hunt a rough country, he purchased from Cornwall. He moved the kennels from 'Furzey Lawn' to his home at Tatchbury and recruited Sam Powell from the **South Wilts Hunt** as his huntsman; his whippers-in were Thomas Jennings and Job Dyer.

In his first season sport was most successful, although the support was not as strong as promised for he in fact only received £500 of the £750 promised subscription. At the end of the season he offered to hunt hounds in the following year for two days a week on the existing subscription advising, "that he felt it most desirable for sport, and hunting the country properly, that it should be hunted three days a week. However, he could only undertake to do this if the sum of £600 was subscribed". He, "also took the opportunity of saying, that if any other party came forward to hunt the country on a more extended scale he would be willing to retire and subscribe liberally to the same".

FINANCIAL PROBLEMS

Hunt records show that this financial problem was to re-occur regularly throughout Mr Timson's term of office. However, he did continue to hunt the country three times a week until 1860, so one assumes that finance was somehow found. Sam Powell left after the first year, and was replaced with John Dinnicomb — "a quiet man with hounds, and having seen some service prior to coming to the Forest serving with Lords Gifford and Parker, and also the **V.W.H.** and the **Puckeridge"**. In 1857 William Hawtin succeeded John Dinnicomb, coming from the **Bedale**.

Mr Timson's stud contained three favourite "nags", *Barbariska, Acorn* and *Cupid*; he not only hunted this trio but also raced them as well.

Hunting throughout Mr Timson's time was good and he was a popular figure so that when he finally decided to resign in 1860 a well attended dinner was held at 'The Crown Inn', Lyndhurst, to present him with a piece of plate to the value of £110; a sum which had been subscribed by the grateful members. Captain William Morant immediately signified his willingness to take the hounds, which arrangement "met with the entire approval of the meeting", according to a note made by the Hon. Sec., Mr Henry Martin Powell. Mr Morant was the youngest son of Mr John Morant of 'Brockenhurst House', and had been a Captain in the Grenadier Guards.

CAPTAIN MORANT

He removed the kennels back to 'Furzey Lawn', keeping William Hawtin on as kennel-huntsman. Captain Morant hunted the hounds himself with Job Dyer as his whipper-in for the first two seasons. After this William Hawtin's son 'Will' turned hounds to him.

The Hunt uniform which had previously been a forest green coat with black velvet collar was changed at this time to the one still in use today. That is a scarlet coat with green collar, worn with a green waistcoat. It is also worth noting that the Hunt Club held its meetings and dinners at 'The Crown Hotel', Lyndhurst, almost exclusively from 1803 until fairly recently, although during Mr Morant's time dinners were also held monthly during the season there.

Hunting was interrupted during December and January of his first season due to severe frosts, but on 16th February a fine run was reported in *Bell's Life*. They met at Picket Post and found their second fox at Burley Anderwood. He went away to Vinney Ridge, through Gillet's Enclosure, by Mark Ash back to Burley and, strange to say, for three successive times he ran this same ring; the third time he broke away through Gillet over a boggy bottom by Bank to Hunt Hill Enclosure where, after one hour and twenty minutes hard running without a check after a regular race, hounds killed him. Seven only saw the end of this run — Captain Morant M.F.H., Captain M. Powell, Captain Boultbee, Mr Timson, Mr Everett, William Hawtin, the kennel-huntsman, and Job Dyer, the whip.

DEATH OF THE HUNT CHAIRMAN

In June, 1865, Mr Andrew Robert Drummond, who had served as Chairman for over twenty years, died at the age of seventy years to the great sorrow of all members. He, like his father before him, had been a great supporter of the N.F.H. and at a dinner held only two months before his death made a speech in which he said he hoped that, in spite of his current infirmity, he would often be enabled to meet the members of the N.F.H. and, "he trusted that there would always be a pack of Foxhounds in the New Forest, for he considered foxhunting a part of the British Constitution". The duties of Chairman were taken over by Mr H.C. Paulet, later Sir Henry Paulet.

In April 1865 a portion of the northernmost country was loaned to the **Tedworth**. Captain Morant resigned after eight seasons, his hounds going to Mr Samuel Nicolls at the **Hursley** (son of the New Forest M.F.H. of the same name), and in 1869 Mr William Cecil Standish took on the hunting of the country.

Sir Reginald Graham, a subsequent Master, said of Mr Morant, "He was a very silent man, who rode the Forest very well. I always looked upon him as the best Forest Huntsman I ever saw".

WILLIAM STANDISH

Mr Standish had previously been Master of the **Hursley** since 1862 and lived at 'South Stoneham House', near Swaythling. Upon becoming M.F.H. of the New Forest he took up residence at 'New Park', Brockenhurst, and also kennelled hounds there. However, I understand that 'Furzey Lawn' kennels were also used from time to time when it was more convenient to do so.

When he was only twenty-two years old, in 1843, Mr Standish had founded a pack of hounds in Pau (France), and since then had hunted with the **Hambledon** and the **Hursley** before taking on the Mastership of the latter.

He was a wealthy man and he spared no expense to show good sport. He and his hunt servants were extremely well mounted, and everything was done very well. He was incredibly patient with hounds, leaving them to work things out for themselves for very long periods which did not suit some of the members. Summers was the kennel-huntsman during this time.

During the winter of 1874 he became ill and so decided to resign. A sale was held at 'Furzey Lawn' and the hounds going to Ireland fetched £1,350. The seven horses made just under £1,000 which was considered to be a handsome sum at the time. Mr Standish died a few years after giving up the Mastership, and prior to his death expressed his wish to be buried in the cemetery overlooking Boltons Bench — a favourite meet.

THE COUNTRY

Mr Lawrence Cumberbatch was the deputy surveyor at that time, and was a keen supporter and Hunt Club member. "He was fond of all sport, but a foxhunter first of all and was held in great esteem by all who knew him." He had responsibility under the Crown for the whole area which comprised some 66,000 acres surrounded by large estates. These were as follows:

On the south side there was 'Beaulieu', an estate of 8,000 acres belonging to Lord Henry Scott (later Lord Montague), and 'Cadlands' which belonged to the Drummond family. To the south-west, 'Exbury' where Sir George Stucley lived, and 'Hinton Admiral', the home of Sir George Meyrick. To the west 'Bisterne', the heavily wooded estate belonging to Mr John Mills who had a dashing little pack of harriers. To the east there was 'Paultons', Mr Sloane-Stanley's property; and 'Embley Park' the home of the Nightingale family. Then there was 'Broadlands', occupied at that time by Mr Cowper Temple. Of course in the heart of the country was Mr Henry Compton's estate known to all foxhunters in the Forest simply as 'The Manor'. Other estates within the country were 'Testwood', the home of the Chairman of the Hunt, Sir Henry Paulet; 'Castle Malwood' where lived General Parker; 'Foxlease' was owned at that time by Captain Buckworth Powell. Mr Bradburne of 'Lyeburn' was a noted supporter, as were the Morant family of 'Brockenhurst Park'. 'Northerwood' at Lyndhurst was occupied by Lord Londesborough during the hunting season at this time. He was very short sighted and had to have a pilot in order to hunt at all.

HUNTING DIARY 1854-1874

10th February, 1857

"Hounds found in Mr Stanley' plantations and hunted steadily up to Crow's Nest. They then raced their fox for 40 minutes by Bramshaw Telegraph, to Eyeworth Wood near the Royal Oak, and Fritham to Stoney Cross across to Pug Pit* where they marked to ground. Dinnicomb hunted the hounds well."

Taken from *Sporting Reminiscences of Hampshire*, by "Aesop".

19th November, 1859

"A fine hunt took place on this day from Stairley, owned by that great preserver of foxes the Duke of Buccleugh. Found at Kings Copse and ran over Hartford Heath, along the Ipley River to Ferney Croft, across the plain to Deer Leap and into the Langley Manor coverts back to Ipley and Black Down to Denny Wood where, as it was getting dark, hounds were whipped off after 20 miles. The following gentlemen were noted as being well up in this hunt: Mr Cumberbatch, Sir Henry Paulet, Captains Heath, Martin and Buckworth Powell, Mr A. Gore, Mr Palmer, Mr Shrubb and Mr Carter. The Huntsman was always well in his place and stayed with hounds throughout this long run.

Taken from *Bell's Life of London*.

March 1874

"Although I have hunted for 40 years and might be called the oldest inhabitant in the country, I cannot recall so good a season as this. When two or three days frost came in the middle of February there were few who could grumble. Rest, indeed, might well have been wanting in many stables."

Taken from *Baily's Magazine* by "C.P."

March 1874

"There has been a succession of excellent sport in the New Forest since the frost went and notably one day in particular, which has been a good deal talked about and will probably be the 'run of the season'. On Saturday, February 16th they found in Lord Henry Scott's woods at Beaulieu and came away over the best parts of the Forest and killed on the Banks of The Southampton Water, near Eling. The second whip waded down hoping to secure some remnant of the fox for a trophy and narrowly escaped drowning in the mud."

Taken from *Baily's Magazine* by "Our Van".

* Now known as Puckpits.

7

The Fast Ladies

1874–1885

Figure 7.1 Sir George A. Meyrick, M.F.H.

Master of the New Forest Hunt from 1878-1885. Shown here at a spring meet at 'Northerwood', Lyndhurst, c. 1879.

(*Courtesy*: Hampshire Record Office, *photo*: Mr Prenderbeigh)

CHAPTER 7

The Fast Ladies

1874–1885

SIR REGINALD GRAHAM

In his book *Foxhunting Recollections*, Sir Reginald Graham explains how he came to be Master of the New Forest Hounds. Apparently he had come down to the Forest to see Lord Wolverton's pack of bloodhounds when they visited during April 1874. He records that their celebrated performance was somewhat lacking in the Forest, "They did not like the thick undergrowth in the New Enclosure, nor did they enjoy the tracts of heatherland; and if there was any noise or the whip used they were apt to turn very sulky for the rest of the day. I remember the first time they were out, Lord Wolverton cried out to a young sportsman who popped his whip, 'For heavens sake don't crack your whip or every one of them will go straight home'."

The trip was not entirely wasted however, as whilst he was in the Forest he heard quite by chance that Mr Standish was giving up hounds and had indeed already agreed to sell his pack to Ireland. The Chairman, Sir Henry Paulet, offered him the country and he "jumped at the offer". He purchased the **Craven** pack of seventy couple for £500; they were apparently for sale due to some internal disagreement in the Hunt. Mr Henry Chaplin of the **Blankney** also gave him some eighteen couples. He weeded the pack down to about fifty couples during the summer and engaged Jack Goddard as kennel-huntsman and first whip, and Jim Reynolds from the **North Hereford** as second whip. He hunted hounds himself.

GOOD EARLY SPORT

He began cubhunting on 11th August but as the mornings were terribly hot he decided to try hunting during the afternoon, meeting at 2.30 or 3 p.m. and going on as long as daylight lasted.

He records that the experiment worked out well as it was seldom as hot at this time in the afternoon as it was at seven or eight in the morning, and every hour they stayed out it got cooler. The *Baily's* hunting correspondent advised that, owing to the good summer, there were huge quantities of falling leaves and this was in turn causing bad scenting conditions. Nevertheless, some good runs were recorded in November that year. On the 10th they met at Stoney Cross. The bitch pack was out and found in Kings Garn; ran to Ravensnest; back by Canterton and Shave Green to 'Manor House'; then over by Acres Down, Pound Hill, onto Ferney Knap and Markway Bridge where they lost him. The hunt lasted one and a half hours and held a very fast pace the whole time. Very few of the field were up at the end.

On the 19th they met at 'The Vine Inn' at Ower. Having drawn blank during the morning, hounds found late in the afternoon in Shelley's Bog, and hunted a ringing fox for about three hours around 'Paultons' and 'Embley', finally accounting for him on Romsey Common. They hacked back to the kennels by moonlight.

VISIT OF THE DUKE OF BEAUFORT

In April 1875 Sir Reginald invited the Duke of Beaufort to bring his hounds down for April hunting. The Duke sent down about twenty couples of doghounds to 'Furzey Lawn' under the charge of Charles Hablin. Lord Worcester hunted them.

The social scene was sparkling. The Duke stayed with his sister, Lady Rose Lovell, at 'Hinchelsea Manor'. Lyndhurst was positively bursting at the seams with "the hunting ton" and at the first meet at Fritham on 15th April, there were about 500 people out on horseback, and probably an equal number out in carriages. Hunting was "capital" during the week and a report of some of the runs will be found in the Hunting Diary section at the end of this chapter.

A local newspaper report of the second meet makes interesting reading.

"The Duke of Beaufort's Hounds, which have been brought into the Forest for a few days hunting, followed up the large meet at Fritham on Thursday, with a really grand gathering at Balmer Lawn, Brockenhurst, on Monday. The news of the presence of this famous pack in the New Forest Country, had been quickly noised abroad and the little village of Brockenhurst was on Monday the centre of a gathering of the elite of sportsmen from this and adjacent countries. Every train arriving from East or West brought with it a long string of horse boxes. The Isle of Wight also contributed its quota via Lymington and accompanying these was a concourse of Lords, Ladies and Gentlemen such as is rarely witnessed, especially in a small country village. For quite an hour before the time announced for the meet the roads in every direction converging on the Lawn were lined with vehicles, horses and persons on foot until, when noon had arrived there were not less than two thousand people present, the horsemen and women alone numbering some six or seven hundred. Lord and Lady Londesborough and party came from Northerwood House in a drag and four-in-hand, and the drags of Mr E.G. Dalgety (Lockerley Hall), Mr Rowland Cooper, Lymington, and others were also present. The Duke of Beaufort arrived soon after twelve, accompanied by Mr Lovell, with whom and Lady Rose Lovell he had been staying at Hinchelsea. Among those on horseback or in carriages we noticed the Marquis of Worcester (who hunts the pack), Lord Arthur Somerset (his brother), General Lord Strathnairn, Lord Algernon St. Maur, Lord Vivian, Lord Eslington, Sir Reginald Graham (Master of the New Forest Hunt), Sir Henry Paulet, General Parker, the Hon. H.D. Curzon, Mr W.J. Long (Master of the Hambledon Hounds), Mr H. Deacon (Master of the H.H.), Mr John Harvey (Master of the Isle of Wight Hounds), Mr H.T. Jenkinson, Mr N.B. Smith, Mr R.C. Bassett, Colonel Reynardson, Miss and Master Reynardson, Mr Lambton, Mr Gervis, Capt. Waterhouse, Captain Powell Montgomery, Mr Merthyr Guest, Dr Hearne, Mr Wilder, Mr Smith (Christchurch), Capt.

Martin Powell, Mr Henry Compton, Mr Charles Day, Mr C. Shrubb, Mr W.C.D. Esdaile, Mr E. Holloway, Mr Duplessis, Mrs de la Tour, Miss Carr, Mrs Stewart, Mr W. Farr, Mr L. Cumberhatch, Mr Hay Morant, Mr Cecil Dixon, Mr H. Day, Mr C. Bovill Smith, Mr Hasler, Mr W. Greenwood, Mr F. Bailey, Mr W.B. Mudge, and many others.

"The field was the most numerous and fashionable ever remembered, even by those who carry their recollections back to the 'deer days', when the Forest was the 'happy hunting-ground', and the perfect paradise of all true sportsmen. The pack started at half-past twelve, and the departure from the meet presented a sight rarely seen, and which will never be forgotten by those who witnessed it. The weather was of the finest, though somewhat too hot for hunting; still, it tended to render the day thoroughly enjoyable to all present. The hounds were taken to the enclosure adjoining New Copse, from whence a fox was quickly halloed across the railway into Park Hill Enclosure. He ran first as if for Stubby, but, being headed by foot people, turned to the left, and came on to Balmer Lawn at the Brockenhurst end of it; then bearing to the right, went as if for New Park, but turned before reaching the road, and, running parallel with it, went into Park Hill Enclosure again, at the Lyndhurst end. He came quickly out and went into Park grounds, where he dodged about for some time, and although viewed once or twice dead-beat, he managed to get to ground, or into a drain in the cover adjoining Pond Head, and was lost. A second fox was not found until five in the afternoon in Ipley Gorse, when he ran down Ipley Water, nearly to Hatched Gate, turned to the right, and going through the adjoining covers ran up Culverly Water, and passed Culverly Farm, crossed the Beaulieu Road, and running through the thickly-timbered Forest adjoining, went into Frame Heath. Turning to the left he ran the length of it, and out near the Lady Cross; went into the New Enclosure beyond, and through it nearly to the edge of Beaulieu Heath, and running short back retraced his steps nearly to Frame Heath, leaving which to the left he kept the thickly-timbered ground nearly as far as Pennerley brush. The time occupied in this run was about fifty-five minutes, and although the pace was at no time good, the scent being flashy and wanting altogether in the Enclosures, yet it gave the hounds an opportunity of showing their qualities, which they did to perfection. Excellent sport had also been obtained during the last and previous week with both the New Forest Deerhounds and the New Forest Foxhounds. The latter pack, hunted by Sir Reginald Graham, had an extraordinary fast run of about an hour to ground at Knightwood on Saturday, the 17th April."

GOOD HUNTING

That summer of 1875 Sir Reginald was able to declare that he was, "delighted with his first season in the Forest, as sport had been so good, hounds had turned out so well and the little pack of bitches had long earned the name of the Fast Ladies". They were composed of those hounds that he had got from the **Craven** and **Blankney**. The latter with a strong *Bentinck* influence, were apparently the more reliable but they were all hard runners and went at a tremendous pace.

In the second season with Charles Hawtin as kennel-huntsman (Jack

Goddard having left to go to the **Blankney**), cubhunting began on 3rd September and finished on 25th April, 1876. They hunted eighty-nine days and the tally was forty-seven foxes. The Master recorded that all through the winter there was a succession of good sport, and although it was wild, cold weather and they were stopped from hunting on twelve days by snow, it was the best season he had in the Forest. The only sad thing was the death of the kennelman William Andrews, "a very good fellow".

THE BEST DAY'S HUNTING

On 14th February Sir Reginald tells of, "the best days hunting I ever had in the Forest or anywhere else. The meet was advertised at Brockenhurst Bridge at eleven. Snow was falling heavily and there was a lot of it on the ground early in the morning. I never dreamed there could be any hunting at all that day and stopped the hounds from going on; but about twelve o'clock there was a bit of a change and I got to the meet at about 1.30 pm, to find that nearly everyone had gone home except about half-a-dozen, one of whom was Sir Claude de Crespigny. The snow was going fast and I was persuaded to draw so we trotted down to Mr Morant's coverts at 'Brockenhurst Park', where, to my surprise we found directly and raced away to Boldre; then by Stockley, Frame, Pigbush and back by the big Enclosures at Woodfidley and Denny, running the rides the whole way, and caught him close to 'Denny Lodge' after 55 minutes. Such a scent, and they ran as if they were tied to him for the whole way, I never saw anything so fast before or since. Sir Claude and I were the only two at the finish, and he helped me to get hounds back to the kennels, for both the whippers-in were lost, and so was everyone else. Although this was far the best thing of the season I had some regret about what had happened, for I felt that if, in spite of the snow, I had gone to the meet an hour sooner (as I ought to have done), probably most of my field would have shared the sport".[1]

FINAL YEARS AS MASTER

Up to 1876 Sir Reginald had lived at 'Jessamine Cottage', Lyndhurst, but on 24th July that year he married and the happy couple moved to 'Fritham Lodge', just north of Stoney Cross with wonderful views all over the Forest.

The next season began badly as Charles Hawtin died suddenly after a short illness. He was aged thirty-eight and was a much respected huntsman with a voice and manner with hounds "such as one seldom sees, in one's life". He was buried at Emery Down Churchyard. Another blow that season was the death of Mr Henry Compton, that great friend and supporter of the N.F.H., as indeed all his family were.

In place of Charles Hawtin, Sir Reginald engaged Alfred Mandeville, and, with Walter Primmer as second whipper-in, they achieved a tally of forty-seven foxes. After a hard season which ended on 11th April '78, Sir Reginald gave up the country and sold his hounds. The smart little bitch pack went to his successor, Mr George Meyrick of 'Hinton Admiral', and the doghounds partly to Lord Spencer of the **Pytchley** and partly to Lord Howth at **Pau.**

Sir Reginald ends his reminiscences of the New Forest with the following remarks.

"I have never seen any country where at times hounds ran harder than in the Forest; this was by no means an every day occurrence. In the autumn the scent is often very moderated and especially so when the leaf is falling; but when that is over, things begin to improve and from January to May — sometimes when the country is almost under water, or sometimes when the ground is as hard as iron — I have seen many days on which hounds can race from morning until night; especially with a straight fox who runs rides in the Enclosures and tracks on the open heath. Those are the days to ascertain whether your hounds have got drive or not, and to my mind they are not much use without it. I have nothing but the most pleasant memories of those happy hunting grounds in the New Forest, and my thoughts can still linger in a vision, of those delightful spring mornings when I drew Matley Bog, and did not draw in vain."

Sir Reginald was the son of the celebrated Sir Bellingham Graham, who has been mentioned in an earlier chapter, and had been entered into fox-hunting at a very early age. He was the friend and pupil of Lord Henry Bentinck, and had been master of the **Cotswold** from 1871-1873, a bad fall causing him to resign. His father had been master of the **Quorn**, **Atherstone** and **Badsworth,** as well as the **Hambledon** for a very short time in 1821, prior to 'Squire' Osbaldeston taking on the country.

MR GEORGE MEYRICK

When Sir Reginald Graham gave up the country in 1878, Mr George Meyrick, a young local sportsman did not hesitate. Although aged only twenty-three years he stepped in immediately with an offer to take over and hunt the country on five days a week, virtually at his own expense. He was accepted with alacrity.

In addition to Sir Reginald's bitches he purchased large drafts from the **Grafton** and other kennels. He took back the outlying parts of the country which had been loaned to adjacent hunts and set up a lavish kennel administration. The house at 'Furzey Lawn', close to the kennels, was built by Mr Meyrick as a hunting box. When one considers that he hunted five and sometimes six days a week in every month except June this must have been almost essential. On three days a week Mr Meyrick hunted hounds himself and on the remaining days Fred Orbell, the kennel-huntsman carried the horn. The whippers-in were Fred Enever, 1st, and Jack Raby, 2nd.

FINE STYLE

Because he had taken over all the original country the distances they had to cover were enormous, but Mr Meyrick and his staff were all well mounted, and no day was too long. "To do the thing properly" was a passion with him, no expense was spared and nothing was too much trouble for his youthful enthusiasm.

In April '79, towards the end of his first season, *Baily's Magazine* advises:

"There have been some good runs with the New Forest Hounds. On Tuesday, 1st April they met at Picket Post; Mr Meyrick who was hunting the hounds, proceeded to draw below Burley Beacon, which unfortunately was

Figure 7.2 A Fine Master — Sir George A. Meyrick.

blank; but in the bog on the left hand side of the Ringwood and Romsey Road, a fox was viewed, and Mr Meyrick soon got the hounds on the line. They ran through Roe Plantation up to the right through Milkham over Brately Plain and Ankercomb Bottom, across Ridley Plain to Backley's Enclosure. The fox here being hard pressed turned short back from Oakley and was run into the open on Bushey Bratley: time, one hour and ten minutes and I never saw anything faster. Amongst those who ran well up when the fox was run into were Mr Meyrick and his sister Miss Meyrick, Fred Enever 1st Whip; Mrs Fawcett, Dr Stevens, Mr Esdaile, farmers Tuck and Bennett and several other hard riding farmers from the neighbourhood, all of the right sort who can, and do go, and who don't press hounds when at fault or drive them over the line. There was a second run that day from Oakley to Brockenhurst, a hunt of one and a half hours. Hounds worked well all day."

The members were very happy indeed with the season's sport; the tally was twenty-eight brace and Alfred turned the hounds out in very good condition.

In the 1879-80 season, sport continued to be good although affected badly by adverse weather conditions. "This has been a terribly disappointing season for hunting men. Frost set in early and operations were brought to a standstill in November, just as horses were in condition and hounds beginning to run well together. Luckily a rapid thaw brought a happier state of affairs after skating had been in full swing for more than a month, and hunters were beginning to despair. Some had taken to skating for something to do, but as a young sportsman put it, 'We must forgive them, for frost has a terribly demoralising effect, and the best of us lose all sense of self-respect at such times'. The skaters had it all their own way until the evening of 27th December and then soft winds and rain prevailed, causing such a rapid thaw that hounds were out on Monday 29th," and again, "There has been a very bad scent in the New Forest as there are such quantities of dead leaves, but the hounds have worked well and have run well in the open, and the young entry are showing well to the front."[2]

SPRING CROWDS

During the years of Mr Meyrick's Mastership, it was the "spring hunting" that brought the crowds of hunting men and, in ever increasing numbers, the ladies. Come April, when hunting had finished in farming countries, the Forest attracted the famous, and the not-so-famous, all with one aim — to make the most of the end of the season. A plethora of hunting writers in the periodicals of the day, write of the hunts and the problems.

"To go safely over the Forest a horse must be quick on his legs in case of difficulties from bogs or ruts, which are often hidden by heather. Those who take their own horses down will find two or three sufficient to see a lot of sport, as the distances to the meets are not great from Brockenhurst or Lyndhurst. Those who have stayed at Brockenhurst speak well of the 'Rose & Crown'. Other quarters may be found at Ringwood, Lymington or Southampton but these are wide. Lyndhurst is the most central, and there we made our headquarters at 'The Crown'. The art of making a sportsman comfortable at the end of a long day is well understood here so no more need be said of Mr Palmer or his staff. Horses are well done too; personal experience can vouch for one mare going well three days a week. To do this requires good corn and lots of it, yet charges are moderate. Mr Pidgeon, too, has a lot of hunters that know the forest, and capital stabling at the 'Forest Inn', Emery Down; a charming spot for a few sportsmen to take up their abode for the season. For London men, to whom time is an object, it is quite possible to run down by the 8.05 from Waterloo, having a horse at the 'Railway Hotel' Lyndhurst, or Brockenhurst, arriving at 11 o'clock in time to get to the 12 o'clock meets, and back again by the 6.50 that same evening, arriving 9.49 in town. This makes a long day, however, and the best way to do it is as we did. Having telegraphed for rooms and stabling at 'The Crown' we went down by the 5.45 arriving at 8.28 at Lyndhurst Road Station, on Wednesday, April 13th, a lovely moonlight night; so with a man to meet the horses it was a pleasant ride along the Forest roads, about three miles to the hotel. Lyndhurst was very full of sportsmen . . . the foxhound kennels being but a short ride from the village. Of course we found our way there more than once during our visit. Close by Mr Meyrick has built a pretty little hunting box where he can stay when too late to get home. They have had a rare season, bringing to hand thirty-seven brace. The pleasure of a day on the flags is second to a day's hunting but here the enjoyment was doubled, being able to look over a pack of hounds whilst strolling about the beautiful woods surrounding the kennels, chatting with Hawtin, hearing tales of his favourites, while he and Raby walked them out after feeding. Bone and muscle has been the maxim here ever since John Warde, who hunted the Forest early in the century. Light-bred hounds could never stand long days in such rough country, and without music no-one could ride to them. It puzzles a stranger to know how enough hounds can be kept together to kill a fox when there is more than one afoot . . ." The author, "Dragon", finishes by giving a very useful piece of advise about the bogs, ". . . avoid them at all costs," he says, "but even more important, if you have a railway journey afterwards never go without a change of clothing; bogs, if they are not dangerous, are wet".[3]

In 1883 a supporter, Stephen Carter, was thrown from his horse near Boltons Bench and killed. He was buried at Eling Churchyard and many of the Forest sportsmen attended the funeral.

In 1884 a cloud hung overhead; for Mr Meyrick who had been a most energetic M.F.H. showing capital sport and improving the pack year by year, took to himself a wife, Jacinta, and decided to resign the Mastership. He had his last day as Master on Tuesday, 21st May, 1885 and as one of the keenest said, "We should all be wearing crape on our arms today". There was a very large field and the bitch pack soon found a fox near the Rifle Butts. They ran him towards the village but he was headed and was caught on top in the garden of local artist Jack Emms.

Emms was a keen supporter and painted many delightful studies of the hounds, horses and meets. Unfortunately, most of these are now housed as part of a major collection in Australia, but there are some still to be seen in the Forest. Mr Peter Green at 'Minstead Manor' has a lovely collection of Emms's studies of hounds, and several portraits. There is a lovely portrait of the M.F.H. cheering hounds on in the dining room at 'The Compton Arms Hotel', Stoney Cross.

That last season had been a triumph, with many famous visitors — Lord Londesborough had taken 'Northerwood' again with his son, Hon. Francis Denison, and their home was an open house to visiting sportsmen such as the Duke of Beaufort, Lord Worcester, Lord Lonsdale and many, many others. Often the field was over 200 at favourite meets. The tally was twenty-five brace, and a further twenty were run to ground. They were stopped on that season for six days due to weather. So, the Mastership was advertised and Mr Meyrick was consulted as to who should come after him. "I don't know" he replied, "the only two men who could afford to as far as I can see, are my saddler and my corn merchant".

No-one, however, came forward and in June a correspondent noted the fact that the country was still vacant. "This is a country that should commend itself to an aspirant for honours as M.F.H., for it is well stocked with foxes and generally holds a scent. There are good walks for puppies and flesh is plentiful, so it is easy to raise a pack of hounds; nor is it an expensive country to hunt. Stable expenses are not high, for screws, if sound in the wind, improve their legs on such soft ground and get through a lot of work if they are never allowed time to go lame. The subscription list is being improved, and all particulars can be obtained from the Hon. Treasurer, Colonel Martin Powell of Lyndhurst. Should no-one come forward a committee will be formed to carry on the hunt but it is hoped that the snug little hunting box near the kennels will soon shelter another sportsman as keen as the one who has just left it."

ZENITH OF THE HUNT'S FAME

There is no doubt that this was the zenith of foxhunting in the Forest, in terms of the size of fields, the social popularity and the place the hunt occupied nationally. *Horse and Hound* was hardly ever without a lengthy weekly report and "Hunting in the Forest" took second place only to "Hunting in the Shires".

April 1885 was abnormally warm — so warm indeed that iced champagne was served at the lawn meets held to entertain the spring visitors, whose numbers expanded daily, as all the other countries finished their seasons.

The Hunt Ball, naturally, was another way of entertaining this wealth of "first rank and fashion", and then, of course, there were the Lyndhurst Races.

LYNDHURST RACES

How many people I wonder, know that "The Racecourse" really **was** a racecourse? The following is a report of a typical meeting in 1885.

"We had a jolly day on the Racecourse on April 25th. A very pretty course was laid out, just like a miniature Ascot, with lines of carriages, and a grandstand, with Wilshier, who knows everyone, on the gate! The grandstand seems to accommodate anyone who is anyone among the New Forest Sportsmen and Ladies. Whilst the total number attending the races could not have been less than 4,000 with all the fun of the fair.

In the first race, the grey entire* belonging to that sporting grocer, Mr Strange, was just pipped at the post, and as this was the local favourite there were many gloomy faces about. Luncheon was most hospitably served, between races, from the carriages . . ."

HUNTING DIARY 1874-1885

16th January, 1875

"On the 16th January 1875 we met at Hilltop Gate, and after drawing a lot of woodlands blank in the morning we at last found a capital good fox at Abbotstanding, and ran a great pace across the open forest to Langley Manor and then on to Southampton Water: up to this about fifty minutes. The fox lay down on the mud, and the hounds could not reach him without sinking step by step as they got nearer to him. There were sixteen couples of doghounds out, and it was getting dusk. I was engaged to dine that night at Minstead Manor House with Mr Henry Compton, so I left and told Jack to get hold of the fox if he possibly could. That evening, rather late, as the party were coming out of the dining-room, a footman came up to me and said, 'They have sent up from the kennels to say that they got the fox after all, and Manager brought home the head'. The genial squire said to me, 'If we had only got that message five minutes sooner we would have opened another bottle of claret'."

"On 30th March met at Stoney Cross. Found at Lucas' Castle, and ran him over to Ocknell and back to the enclosure at Pugpits, where we lost him. Found at King's Garn, and ran him by Lynwood, Bramshaw, Ocknell, Broomy, to Islands Thorns, where the fox was just before us and quite done. As we went into the last enclosure a lot of young horses which were tuned out in the Forest galloped into the middle of the pack. This gave the fox a chance, and we lost him after one hour twenty minutes, most of it at tremendous pace, without any check all the way."

Taken from *Foxhunting Recollections* by Sir Reginald Graham.

Saturday, 11th March, 1876

"The meet was at New Park. Sir Reginald Graham has again shown us grand sport with a Brockenhurst fox, this time with the dog pack. After a longish draw, not finding till three o'clock, a splendid fox went away from New Copse, through Perry Wood, taking a good line for Brockenhurst Manor, but, for reasons best known to himself, turned sharp to the right across the railway, to Whitley, circling back through New Copse, Lady Cross, Frame and Hawk Hill, on to Beaulieu Heath, heading right away for Norley, across Norley Farm, onto the Heath again, the hounds rolling over their fox dead beat in the open, within fifty yards of Norley Wood. The run lasted one hour and a half, with hardly a check. The country was terribly heavy, and the pace from Hawk Hill very fast— in fact, I think, quite as severe as our run from Brockenhurst on February 14th with the 'ladies', when we killed near Denny Lodge. Out of a field of about thirty, only seven were up at the finish,

*Un-cut stallion

namely, the Master, Lord Henry Scott, M.P., Sir Claude de Crespigny, Messrs Powell-Montgomery, Duplessis, Emms and the second whip. Since the melancholy death of his kennel huntsman, Sir Reginald is only able to take out one whip, Charles Hawtin, temporarily doing duty at the kennels. At our Hunt meeting today (14th), to the great satisfaction of the whole Hunt, Sir Reginald expressed his willingness to continue hunting the country."

6th November, 1877

"Red-letter days have been rare, if not altogether unknown, with any packs of foxhounds thus far in this somewhat remarkable, or rather unremarkable, season. The run with the New Forest, of which I am now going to endeavour to give a description, if it did not occur on a day which deserves the name of a red-letter one, must at least be considered as extraordinary in more senses than one, even if we eliminate the sensational element from it altogether. Let me first point out that the New Forest Foxhounds are kept at Furzey Lawn, near Lyndhurst, Hampshire, and that the Master is Sir Reginald Graham, who has for his whips Alfred Mandeville and Walter Primmer. The nearest towns of approach for intending visitors, of whom it is unreasonable to expect there will be many after reading of this run, are Southampton, Lymington, and Ringwood, for the N.F.H. or New Forest Foxhounds.

"The meet was at the Vine Inn at Ower, when, after time allowed for stragglers, and those who have not learned the maxim concerning the early bird and the worm, to join the rendezvous, the order was given for a fast move for Embley. There a find was soon effected, the difficulty of discovering Reynard's whereabouts being surmountable, even by human nostrils, so glorious a scenting morning was it. This fox proved a right gallant one, and worthy of the famous pack at his brush. The coverts at Embley are extensive and the grounds around corresponding, so the fox had plenty of tactics for trial before a permanent vacation of his domains. The scent was so hot, however, and he was raced so hard and persistently up and down his happy hunting-grounds, that he made occasional dashes out on the side towards Romsey, and, finding that no go, he tried another similar venture towards Wellow. Home quarters, however, had now become much too warm for comfort, and Charley discovered that Embley was no longer for him a peaceful abiding place. His next bolt was across the lane and over the fields towards Pauncefote Farm. Thence he turned to the left down through the covert over the Salisbury road to Greenhill, and down into the meadows as if steeplechasing to the Old Abbey Church at Romsey. Here a mob of fellows, who behaved as though they had never seen a real fox before in their lives, and who, as Mr Carter remarks in a provincial paper, 'must have fancied it was some wild foreign animal just escaped from Bostock and Wombwell's menagerie', by their shouting and yelling turned him away again to the left. The point of the fox was evidently Romsey Abbey, but the hullabaloo caused another diversion, and the hounds now raced him fast and furiously the whole way up the meadows to Greatbridge, and pulled him down in fine style in the field adjoining Timsbury Mill. The finish was seen by very few of the well-appointed sportsmen of the morning, and the pace and country were all too trying for any but the most daring and the best mounted. In fact, beyond the Master and the whips, the field was reduced to a respectable unit, in the person of Mr S. Carter of Totton, who claims the credit, and deserves it, of having seen the whole run. As for the rest, they had been shaken off for miles before the finish, and so distanced must they have been, that none of them came to the 'Whoohoop' even after the fox was broken up.

"In this run with the New Forest, no hounds could possibly have stuck more gamely to their fox, and, considering the nature of the country, very few could have gone faster. Though the scent was admittedly of a burning sort, yet it must be remembered that six or seven roads were crossed, a species of hunting which always tries hounds very much, and sometimes causes them to turn up the game altogether, unless there are a few staunch good-nosed ones among their number. It may be easily understood from this how it was that the field were so outrageously 'out of the hunt'. No doubt, however, many a neighbouring Hampshire man 'thinks himself accursed and holds his manhood cheap' to reflect that he was not there to see something, however little, of this run from Embley, which unquestionably is likely to be talked about for many a day to come, or at all events until its fame shall have been eclipsed by a longer and more glorious one. It is common justice to say that Sir R. Graham was with his hounds everywhere, and that he handled them in a most judicious and masterly manner. I hope that, notwithstanding an avoidance of anything like undue laudation or triumphant cracking of the descriptive whip, I have at least rescued this run of the New Forest Fox Hounds from total oblivion, and raised it out of the ruck of provincial records."

Taken from *The Hampshire Chronicle* by "Cerise".[4]

24th January, 1878

"Lord Percy was staying with me to have a look at the north of the country, which he had never seen, and I mounted him on a bay mare called *Gelatine*. We met at the Royal Oak, Fritham, with sixteen couple of doghounds; went first to Islands Thorns, a large enclosure which was full of deer that morning. They gave us some trouble, but I got the hounds together and trotted off a couple of miles to some gorse outside Sloden. An old fox was off like a shot, and we raced him at a rattling pace over the open heath for thirty-three minutes, and caught him between Goreley and Fordingbridge. It was a terrific pace, and when Mr Bradburne got up to us he sang out to me, 'Wherever you go, all your life you will never see such a gallop as that again'. We found another fox in the afternoon at Hasley, but the scent had changed since the morning, and we lost him at Broomy Lodge."

Taken from *Foxhunting Recollections* by Sir Reginald Graham.

1st April, 1879

"There have been some good runs with the New Forest Hounds. On Tuesday 1st they met at Picket Post; Mr Meyrick who was hunting hounds himself, proceeded to draw below Burley Beacon which proved blank; but in the bog on the left side of the Ringwood Cadenham Road, a fox was viewed and Mr Meyrick soon got the hounds on the line. They ran through Roe Plantation, up to the right through Milkham Enclosure over Bratley Plain, Ankercomb Bottom, and Ridley Plain to Backley. The fox being here hard pressed turned short back from Oakley and was run into in the open at

Bushey Bratley. Time, one hour and ten minutes and at times I never saw hounds run faster. The second run on that same day was from Oakley, through Burley Old to Burley New, back to Oakley, across Red Rice Shade up to Wilverly Plantation at a racing pace, without a check at Wilverly, out over Homsley Bog, below Cole's (the keeper) cottage. Time, one hour and a half and the hounds worked well. They have had very good sport this season and have killed 28 brace and several very good runs. Alfred Orbell turns the hounds out in really good condition."

May 1880

"When the hunting season comes to an end, a bitter end, in the grass countries there is still good sport to be enjoyed with horse and hound in the New Forest, where the sound of the horn and the merry cry of hounds may be heard echoing through its beautiful glades during the months of April and May. Perhaps sportsmen from the Shires, accustomed as they are to flying gallops and quick bursts over strong fences might think it tame work riding to hounds where it is sometimes hard to tell which are enclosures and which is open country. And where the principal excitement consists in the avoidance of bogs and low branches of trees under which they are obliged to gallop. Nor would they care to be exiled to such a country throughout the season, but to any true sportsman fond of hounds there is much enjoyment to be found with the foxhounds in the New Forest. In this favoured country where the cry of 'Ware, wheat' is unknown, Mr Meyrick is enabled to begin cubhunting in July and goes on through May, and it is not in every country that a May fox may be hunted. Sportsmen will find good quarters for horse and man at The Crown, at Lyndhurst, from which all meets are within easy reach. Fancy riding out on a fresh spring morning through those beautiful glades and thickets, where birds are singing and the air is scented with gorse and wild flowers. A well bred hack (or anything that is quick on his legs) able to gallop, will do here, there is little or no jumping. You saunter along and it seems too good to be true that hunting is the object of your ride at this time of the year, till he pricks his ears, and quickens his pace and you realise that others are on the road. Arriving at the meet at say Boldrewood there are about a hundred horsemen and a few carriages. Foot people are collected on a hill from which grand views can be seen of the Forest stretching away on all sides. It is a very pretty sight."

September 1881

"There are few counties so favourable as the New Forest for cubhunting, for there are neither crops to be avoided nor fences full of leaf to bring grief to horse or rider. Last to leave off hunting and first to begin, Mr Meyrick is indeed lucky to hunt such a country. From the 3rd of May when they finished the season at Boltons Bench to the 30th August when they commenced hunting (later than usual this year), seems such a short span, and yet the Master managed to make a sporting tour, fishing and shooting big game in Canada and North America returning to hunt his hounds the first day of cub-hunting. The contrast between the hunting in the New Forest at the end of the season and the beginning is striking.

"Where now are the fashionable crowds who are to be seen at the 12 o'clock meets in springtime? Ten or twelve keen sportsmen and two or three young

Figure 7.3 A Hunting Family

Sir George A. Meyrick pictured with his two sisters outside 'Hinton Admiral House', c. 1884.

(*Courtesy*: P.J.P. Green, *photo*: John Tarlton)

ladies comprise the field when the meets are at 4.30 am increasing in numbers perhaps as the hours roll on till there might be twenty or thirty by the time we early risers are ready to go home for breakfast. Though cubhunting involves rising, tubbing and shaving in the dark, by candlelight, anxious all the while that the groom might not have risen to feed and saddle the hunter. But very enjoyable are these mornings, once a start is made, whether the mount is an old and trusted favourite, or a young one that has all to learn. Horses always seem to know when they are going hunting. Gaily they step along until a turn in the road shows that pack jogging along in the front. Now nerves tingle, and merry are the greetings while the huntsman throws a loving but critical eye over the pack; and down in the forest it must be said that the pack have improved this season, for besides having been able to put forward a lot of home-bred hounds Mr Meyrick secured the Duke of Grafton's draft and Frank Beers must have had a good entry to spare such a lot. There is no change in the staff, the Master carries the horn, Will Hawtin is kennel huntsman and 1st whip and Jack Raby is second. With a country so well stocked with foxes it was no surprise that they were able to bring some to hand the first morning, so that the youngsters have entered well and it is a pleasure and a treat to see them hunt."

The above extracts are taken from *Baily's Magazine* by "Our Van".

17th April, 1884

"Saturday was a red letter day with the Foxhounds. Certainly the best day that the writer has ever seen with them.

"Mr Meyrick met at Telegraph Hill where, as might be expected, a large field assembled. With Alfred Orbell as kennel huntsman it need not be said that hounds looked well but the 16 couples of ladies are well worth looking over, and Master and men look ready to begin another season.

"Deadmans Bog was the first draw and clearly deserves renaming Spillman's Bog for an amusing incident. A native sportsman was showing the country to a visitor and explaining where lay the hidden ditches so that he might avoid them. Suddenly someone began to gallop and the visitor cut short the lecture to go out for a voyage of discovery on his own account. With perfect success, for we soon saw his boots performing a sort of wardance in the air, whilst his head was exploring one of those hidden ditches, and his horse, enjoying his freedom would soon have vanished into space had he not recognised a stable companion and stopped to rub noses.

"These spills may be said to make the recipient 'Free of the Forest'. Should there not be some ceremony attached like that of blooding a novice?

"It was exactly one o'clock when *Sylvia* spoke to the line of a fox on Ashley Plain and the Masters cheer brought the pack together and away they raced with a hot scent, up wind.

"Although the wiley one must have been gone some time, they raced over the plain, leaving Ashley Lodge to the right over the bottom, for Island Thorns bearing to the right past Amberwood Cottage through Slodens without dwelling a second, over to Broomie, through it leaving the Lodge on the left, over the heath to Milcombe and into Roe. Only a dozen horsemen with them when they turned to the left for Milcombe again, then bearing right over the heath, they ran hard, *Drosky*, the cup bitch of last year, leading them up for the first time. Charley Fox, the 2nd whipper-in, had viewed some deer along a track a few minutes earlier, but hounds picked out the line of their fox up the track for about a mile to the Ringwood Road by Bushey Bratley where the fox was headed, or perhaps his heart failed him, for he turned short down wind while the deer crossed the road. The field had been rather hard on hounds pressing them up the track and now they came to a check after a sharp gallop of 30 minutes, 6 miles in a straight line. The Master held them down wind into Slufters, hit him off in the corner over the little hidden brook out over the heath, back through the corner of Milcombe again, away for Broomie, where they ran up to a pond and all flashed in like a lot of ducks, so hot and dry were they, and no doubt the fox had also stopped for a drink. Being on his return journey he had kept meeting the stragglers of the field and had laid down in the thick heather. The Master made a capital cast and hit him off in a boggy gully so they worked up to him and he jumped up right under our horses, so close that we had time to look to see that it was the right animal. He was clean from the heather but his back was up and stiff, but he was still full of going and soon eluded his foes before they caught view in the high heather. Away he went into Broomie with hounds on good terms but down wind now, past the Lodge on the left, through Holly Hatch and Anses Wood over a brook at the bottom, where some colts galloped up the hill after him. But hounds carried the line up the hill to the top and Mr Cumberbatch with the others that were following in traps, had viewed him bearing right for Fritham, but bearing left he ran through Amberwood and Alders Hill to Sloden and away for Broomie again, he began to run much shorter and turned to the left and Harry Peckham, the runner with the terriers, viewed him into Sloden. They ran through here to Amberwood again to Island Thorns away over the plain to Ashley Lodge. Ned Teece here jumped some big rails onto the heath, leaving it on the left, up the hill to the road, down which they carried the line past the Stony Quarry to the brook in the bottom, through the old wood and ran into him close to Ashley Lodge at 7 minutes past three. Distance about 18 miles and every hound, 16 couples, up. Were our horses done? Just a little."

Spring Hunting in the New Forest

"Such good sport as natives and visitors have enjoyed here this spring deserves recording in the everlasting pages between these green covers. Year after year, as the best of all seasons draws to a close, sportsmen from all countries gather together to prolong the season they love best in this favoured district. Surely the thanks of all are due to the noble founder of the forest, for to him we are indebted for much sport long before and long after the time that it is possible to pursue the chase in agricultural districts; and the forest is to be enjoyed in many other ways, which are yearly becoming more appreciated by artists and naturalists in search of the picturesque and grotesque in nature, invalids hoping for health, and the brain weary toilers anxious for rest and quiet in pure air and seclusion. All find what they require in the forest; but it is for sport and how sportsmen enjoy themselves that these pages are written, so it may be as well to give some details of what each pack has been doing.

"Many of the regular visitants were kept away this year, and the sudden death of Lady Rose Lovell cast a gloom over the Forest, while the absence of the popular Master of the deerhounds and his charming daughters was lamented by all, though the Hon. Gerald Lascelles, who undertook the onerous duties of Master, hunted the hounds as to the manner born, and showed rare sport, which is here recorded.

"With the foxhounds too there has been a cloud overhead, for Mr Meyrick, who has been a most energetic M.F.H., showing capital sport and improving his pack year by year, has taken to himself a wife and relinquished his first love; and so well have all matters connected with foxhunting been managed under his mastership that everyone seems afraid to follow in his footsteps for fear of failure, and the pack has been dispersed, excepting a few couples that were brought in as a foundation for a new pack, should any M.F.H. come forward. This is a country that should commend itself to an aspirant for honours as M.F.H., for it is well stocked with good wild foxes and generally holds a scent. There are good walks for puppies, and flesh is plentiful, so it is easy to raise a pack of hounds; nor is it an expensive country to hunt.

"Stable expenses are not high, for screws, if sound in the wind, improve their legs on such soft ground and get through a lot of work if they are never allowed time to go lame. The subscription list is being improved, and all particulars can be obtained from the Hon. Treasurer, Colonel Martin Powell, Lyndhurst. Should no one come forward to take the mastership, a committee will be formed to carry on the hunt, but it is to be hoped that the snug little hunting-box near the kennels may soon shelter another sportsman as keen as he who has just left it.

"Lyndhurst on a fine spring morning is like a little Melton when everyone is starting to hunt; not so smart, perhaps, for many visitors wear their oldest garments to finish, and as to hats, they never go back, while most horses have that well-known 'end of the season' look which may be better described as fine-drawn. Merry are the parties that set out from the different hunting quarters, and cordial the greetings as sportsman meet again after a year's separation, for year after year they collect here from all countries, and some are as much at home as the natives themselves. We, who for several years have made the Crown Hotel our head-quarter, are quite at home, for our ways are known and our wants anticipated; and no one values kindly attention more than wet and weary sportsman, for whom the genial Palmer and his able staff spare no trouble. In the stables too our horses are well turned out in the morning, bright and clean as from a private stable, and, as most horses are expected to hunt at least three days a week, Fakes, the stud-groom does not spare the corn-bin! If our own horses are not able to take their turn we requisition one of Palmer's hunters, which are always fit to go and thoroughly know their duties, for they have to carry all sorts and conditions of men and women. Charles Keeping, of Emery Down, has some useful horses on hire, and Marsh of Basingstoke takes down some good hunters to Lyndhurst, so there is plenty of choice.

"Saturday, 11th April, was a really good day with the foxhounds at Picket Post. They found in a gorse brake near Roe and ran nearly to Linwood, turning through Pinwick Wood, over the stream and past Roe Cottage to Broomie and Holly Hatch nearly to Ocknell Pond, over the open to Ocknell Arch; up the road to Boldre Wood and down through Holm Hill and

Holiday's Hill over the road to Gillett's, and away through Mark Ash into Oakley, and back again into Knightwood till they marked him to ground in the great earth at Vinney Ridge, after a run of two hours and twenty minutes. Found another in Burley Roacks and ran hard over the bogs across the Christchurch road to Clumber, racing through Rhinefield, Sandy's, and Vinney Ridge to Warwickslade cutting, where they checked and hunted steadily through Hurst Hill, Whitley Wood across the Brockenhurst road by New Park, and through Hollands Wood to Park Hill and Denny Lodge, down to the bog by the railway; and through Woodfidley, Stubbey, and Pignall to the Victoria Tilery. By this time Mr Meyrick and his whips were alone struggling on, changing horses one with another, and by all accounts taking turn and turn about on Bumpstead's cob, that was requisitioned from the bush barrow; but the sole survivor of the field, Mr Cumberbatch, was not near enough to tell tales, till they stopped hounds near Ramnor at dark, after running one hour and fifty-five minutes. A very hard day for hounds and horses, as it was late before they arrived home.

"Tuesday, the 21st, was a very sad day for the Forest — the last meet of Mr Meyrick's foxhounds at Bolton's Bench, and, as one of the keenest said, 'We should all be wearing crape on our arms today'. There was a very large field, and the lady pack soon found a fox in the bog near the rifle butts. They ran towards the village, where the fox was headed, and made short work of him in Jack Emms's garden, close to the studio, so he may have a spirited picture for next year's Academy. They found another fox in Brockis Hill, and hunted slowly through Busketts, Irons' Hill, and Woodlands, across the road and railway to Deer Leap, where he ran them out of scent.

"The weather turned cold and wet before Friday the 24th, much more like hunting, but there was no sport worthy of record with the deerhounds, for everything seemed to go wrong though they killed a deer late in the evening. On Saturday, the 25th, Mr Mills, of Bisterne, brought his pretty little pack of harriers to Bratley Water, where a goodly field met to see them hunt a fox, which they did right merrily from Sloden, round Islands Thorns and Amberwood, where their merry cry warned him to fly and seek shelter in an earth in the open, near Broomie, after thirty-five minutes; nor were horses sorry when they finished.

"On Wednesday, the 29th, Mr Mills showed the followers of his merry little pack another good run, but scent didn't allow George Sears to handle the fox, which they hunted from Sett Thorns to Lady Cross.

"Had friend Vian only seen the casualties he would have raised the premiums on insurances at 64, Cornhill, for all who hunt in the Forest, but no one ever seems to be hurt, for the falling is generally in soft places.

"On Saturday, the 2nd, Mr Mills had another merry day, though they did not kill a May fox. They met at Ocknell Arch, and found in King's Garn, but did not do much with him, as their attention was diverted by an antlered monarch of the woods, so they went on to the Grove and ran a fast ring over the open to the Wilderness, back to the Grove, where the fox went to ground. Found another in Slufter, and raced over the open to Milkham, down to Broomie, where he too went to ground. Another, that was viewed in Milkham, led them right round the great enclosure, and through it at the thickest part away to Broomie Lodge; through this to the fields, when he turned and ran back to Milkham, so they were stopped late in the afternoon after a very jolly day.

"It may be well to tell of sportsmen that have visited the Forest this season. Lord Londesborough and his son, the Hon. Francis Denison, are always out, and Northerwood is an open house for sportsmen during the season. The Duke of Beaufort, Lord Worcester, Lord Lonsdale, Lord Lewis, the Hon. Edward Portmen, Sir Richard and Lady Clynn, Major Candy, Mr Esdaile, Master of the Somerset, Mr Merthyr Guest, Master of the Blackmore Vales, and many more, have swelled the fields up to two hundred at favourite meets."

The above extracts are taken from *Baily's Magazine* by "Dragon".

NOTES

1 *Foxhunting Recollections* by Sir Reginald Graham.
2 *Baily's Magazine*.
3 Taken from *Baily's Magazine* by "Dragon".
4 "Cerise" was the pen name of Mr Stephen Carter, who was killed out hunting with the New Forest Hunt.

8

The Country Divided

1885–1895

Figure 8.1 Mr Henry Martin Powell, M.F.H.

Master of the New Forest Hunt from 1894-1899 and from 1905-1907. Shown here at a meet near Brockenhurst, c. 1895.

(*Courtesy:* Miss Rachel Pulteney, *photo:* John Tarlton)

CHAPTER 8

The Country Divided

1885–1895

In the event, in spite of advertising in all the well known sporting papers, no-one came forward to follow Mr Meyrick. At a meeting held in July 1885, the committee met to discuss the ongoing situation. Their decision was to split the country into two parts: the Eastern, or main portion to be hunted by a committee, the Western was offered to Mr John Mills of Bisterne, who prior to this date had hunted his delightful little pack of harriers in roughly the same area.

A GREAT SPORTSMAN

The committee then empowered Mr Gerald Lascelles, a leading member of the Hunt Club, and member of the committee to go to the annual hound sales at Rugby to purchase a pack of hounds. They hoped in this way to make the country more attractive to a potential, incoming Master.

Fortunately, many of Mr Meyrick's hounds were still up for sale and the best of them were speedily brought in. These, together with some from the **Burton**, in all some twenty-five couples of bitches, formed the basis of the new pack. In addition Mr Lascelles purchased four couples of doghounds that he particularly liked. Whilst recognising that they would not be suitable for the Forest he used them to trade some weeks later for the types that he wanted.

Mr Lascelles was the Deputy Surveyor of the New Forest, having succeeded Mr Lawrence Cumberbatch in 1880. A noted sportsman in all branches of field sports he wielded immense power wisely and fairly so that no faction ever felt badly treated. Anyone who loves the Forest and who loves hunting should read his book *Thirty Five Years in The New Forest*. Although written in 1915, it is still a positive joy.

His other great love was the sport of falconry, and the falcons from his mews at 'Queen's House', Lyndhurst, were a familiar sight around the steeple of Lyndhurst Church. The tinkling of their bells was a welcome sound to homecoming sportsmen after a long day.

MAJOR BROWNE

To return to the history: cubhunting began, as usual, under the committee but in September Major John Browne came forward with an offer to hunt the country and was accepted.

Major Browne came of an old Hertfordshire sporting family; the Brownes of 'Hall Court' having been well known for their sporting connections for centuries. Indeed, his ancestor Sir Anthony Browne had been Master of the Horse to Henry VIII. Major Browne's father had kept a private pack at 'Hall Court' for many years and Major Browne had acted as whipper-in and huntsman in his younger days. In addition he had been Master of the **South Staffordshire Hunt** for the twelve years prior to his coming to the Forest.

He brought with him a small bitch pack of his own, bred mainly from the **Brocklesby**, **Belvoir** and **Croome** kennels, and together with those hounds bought in at Rugby, a most satisfactory season's sport was enjoyed.

Weather conditions that season were attrocious all over the Kingdom; however, *Baily's* report that Major Browne had been able to hunt often, "when other hounds have been confined to their yards and benches. Major Browne succeeds Mr Meyrick and is just the man for the country having already had good experience of Cannock Chase". In addition to his love of hunting Major Browne had distinguished himself on the racing field. He had won many races riding his own horses: *Hall Court*, who ran in the Grand National four years running; *The Baron*; *Forest Green*; and *Wild Thyme*, all of whom he also personally trained.

It is recorded that his two sons, who sometimes whipped-in to him, astonished members of the Hunt Club by wearing bowler hats with their scarlet coats and top boots!

By the end of the season Major Browne found that the Forest was too much for his failing health and he resigned, returning to 'Hall Court' where he established a small private pack "much to the delight of his neighbours".

SUCCESSION OF MASTERS

He was succeeded by a popular local landowner, Mr Frederick Bradburne of Lyburn. He engaged John Dale as his huntsman for the three seasons he held office. Reports of the hunting enjoyed at that time follow in the Hunting Diary section. A startled member records that at a foggy November meet two distinguished visitors — Lord and Lady Hesketh — were out. Lady Hesketh daringly wearing a scarlet habit which "made some of us quite jump in our saddles when we first caught sight of it".

In 1889 Mr Stanley Pearce of 'Loperwood Manor', Little Testwood near Totton, took over from Mr Bradburne. Will Povey was his huntsman.

Meanwhile, in the eastern portion, Mr Mills, hunting with his smart little pack of "reconditioned" harriers, was showing excellent sport. His huntsman, George Seers, was well known for his excellent control of his hounds and their steadiness. He also had a wonderful knowledge of the Forest. On one occasion, having found a fox in Wilverly, hounds hunted *through hares*, running eventually to Beaulieu Heath where they duly accounted for their fox.

When Mr Mills gave up, Sir John Thursby took over that part of the country with his son George (subsequently to become Master of the Buckhounds) hunting hounds for him.

Mr George Thursby was without doubt the greatest "gentleman jockey" of his day. Among his many great successes on the turf he rode *John 'O Gaunt* into second place in the Derby of 1904 and two years later he took second place again, this time riding *Picton*.

Figure 8.2 A Walking Place

(Taken from an old print, 1886)

Certainly his marvellous riding ability made him "a desperate man to follow in a hard run".

Visiting sportsmen during this period could expect to hunt on six days out of seven with two packs of foxhounds, or the "deerhounds" as they were then known. It was not until earlier this century when they gave up hunting does and hunted the Fallow buck only that the deerhounds became known as the **New Forest Buckhounds.**

A visiting hunting correspondent asked an old local sportsman to tell him exactly how long the season was in the Forest, and received the reply, "Ah, they are sometimes without a cry in June!".

A Clash

In early 1892 an extraordinary clash between the two packs of foxhounds took place. Neither Sir John, nor George Thursby were out on this day, the kennel-huntsman Sam De Ville was carrying the horn.

Both packs having hunted into the same part of the forest just south of Lyndhurst, Mr Pearce's followers had heard the rival pack (for there was great rivalry between the two) getting closer until they finally came together on the same line at the Rifle Butts. The combined packs then ran on along the Brockenhurst Road and into New Park past the buckhound kennels.

The huntsmen of both packs were meanwhile vying with each other, riding with the utmost jealousy, each screaming at his own hounds and each sounding his horn for all he was worth. As they careered past the buckhound kennels, Allen, the buckhound huntsman, rushed out and with great glee joined in the din by halloaing and blowing his horn furiously.

In spite of this, and the complaints of Povey, the whipper-in, who said it was giving him a headache, hounds accounted for their fox in New Park; each huntsman claiming the honours of course!

At this time there was an extraordinarily keen, young, hard-riding crowd of horsemen following hounds. The leaders of this set were subsequently to figure largely in the history of the Hunt. They consisted of the two Powell boys (sons of the Honorary Secretary), the two Heseltine boys, and Tommy Timson. Tommy Timson also had seven sisters riding to hounds, so it may be assumed that this fun was not confined to the male followers! On hunting mornings they used to rise early and build jumps out of brushwood across all the rides in the enclosures where hounds were likely to draw. The next day they would go out and take them all down again. They hoped in this way to erradicate the impression that the main art in hunting the Forest consisted mainly of avoiding the bogs!

POINT-TO-POINT RACES

It was Mr Pearce who was responsible for starting and organising the Hunt Point-to-Point races then held near Totton. He resigned the Mastership in 1894 handing over to Mr Martin Powell, whose father, Colonel William Martin Powell, had been Honorary Secretary to the Hunt for thirty years until 1887. In 1895 Sir John Thursby resigned the Western portion of the country and Mr Powell lost no time in taking it back again. The New Forest Hounds were re-united.

HUNTING DIARY 1885-1895

December 1885

"At last I am happy to tell you that scent has improved and sport accordingly, as the following notes from my foxhunting diary will show.

"On Tuesday, 9th, Major Browne could not leave the kennels till one o'clock, on account of the frost being so hard; but ever keen to show spirit, he met at Boldre Bridge a little after two o'clock, and drew the little coverts close there, but did not find a fox till we got to New Park, where there were three or four afoot, when hounds divided, and three and a-half couples ran a fox across Balmer Lawn through Ramnor, straight to Matley Bog, skirting Deer Leap into Busketts, but they ran him so he did not like to stay, so went on through Fletchwood across the fields to Totton, where George Kennett whipped off at dark, and he alone with them. The rest went away to Rhinefield after running a brace to ground.

"On Friday, 12th, they met at Crowesfield Houses, and found a fox in Plaitford Bog, which went away very sharp straight through Mr Bradburne's, Lyburn, into Pugpits to the Grove, then into Winstead Manor, where they checked and changed foxes. With a very good scent they ran round and round in the Manor and to the Grove, but could not get hold of a fox amongst so many, and went home after a very good day's sport.

"On Saturday, 13th, I rode across to Wilverley Post to meet Mr Mills's pack, and see how George Sear's is getting on. He soon found fox Number 1 under Burley Rocks, and ran through Knightwood to Pugpits, away towards Slufter, turned left-handed, and hounds divided, after running 30 minutes. Fox Number 2 went back to Knightwood, and they marked him to the ground after 15 minutes. Fox Number 3 was found near the Old House in Oakley, and he also went to ground in Knightwood after 30 minutes. Fox Number 4 found near the keeper's house in Oakley, was the hero of the day, as he stood before them for an hour and a half, and beat them at dark, when they were whipped off after a very hard day for hounds and horses."

January 1886

"On Tuesday Major Browne's hounds met at Blackdown Bridge, a meet hitherto unknown in the country, and many were the inquiries as to its whereabouts. Nevertheless a goodly number assembled at twelve at the railway bridge known as Beaulieu Road Station, which, under a disguised, but probably correct name, had set so many old stagers a-thinking. The first draw was Ipley River, without result, then some little gorse covers on the open heath, till at last the hounds went feathering up a little path, and dashed into a patch of gorse on a hillside. Hardly had the leading hounds disappeared when a welcome tally-ho from Mr Ingram let us know that he was already away. The hounds quickly settled to his line, and ran at first as if making for Ipley River, then, turning abruptly to the right, crossed the ground once covered by an extensive gorse, but now unfortunately burnt, and went into Gurney Fields, and straight through this covert and on through the next, over the Beaulieu Road, and headed for the great woodland of Frame. The fox, however, turned to the left, and gave us a spin round Hawk Hill before entering the big woods, which so often get us into trouble.

The Hounds on this occasion drove their fox to Lady Cross where Mr Meyrick, the former Master, is now living, and then turned short back, pointing again for Hawke Hill. Here unluckily the hounds divided, more than one fresh fox being on foot, and at last it became necessary to stop them. Thus ended in disappointment a really good gallop of 40 minutes. The hounds then drew the hodes and the bogs on the open heath towards home, but did not find again."

25th January, 1886 — In The New Forest

"While hunting is impossible in all the hard riding counties we are still able to get along somehow, and enjoy sport even when riding is almost impossible, so our doings may be of interest to others less favourably situated. We go for sport more than for show here so we do not care how hounds are brought out so long as they can run, and perhaps kill a Forest fox.

"Monday 25th, did not look much like a hunting morning when Major Browne sent round to say that he would hunt if possible, but as all the leading sportsmen in Lyndhurst had the same tip no-one could stay in doors, as the meet was to be at The Manor at 12 o'clock. So there we gathered (not on the clippers that stand in the stall at the top, but on general utility nags that are always in condition, and even take a turn in the sledge when wanted). At The Manor the Major was on horseback, and his men — Kennett, father and son — on foot; but it was not long before the little beauties found a fox which after a ring, went away across the fields by Fleetwater to Castle Malwood and Cantertons, back across the fields, to ground in a drain, after a very good run of an hour and a half. The Master then drew back into the Manor, and hounds could not get another fox away, so at two o'clock he decided to go to Busketts, where they found directly, and ran round towards the roads between Lyndhurst and Lyndhurst Road station, as if for Deer Leap when, headed by a wagon, he turned back to the racecourse. At this time only the Master and his son, with young W. Palmer, were riding to hounds and they skirted the bog to the right, crossing the road close to the kennels, across the fields by the Mill, into the small covert close by Acres Down, where young Palmer viewed him, and gave such a rattling view holloa that he frightened his horse and caused an A.O.T. but, nothing daunted, he continued on foot (for it is no use trying to catch a runaway in the forest — better to trust to luck), and he was in luck, for he followed hounds on foot to Emery Down, and met Fakes, the head man at the Crown Hotel exercising *The Gem of the Forest*, so deposed him on the other errand, and followed the hounds to Alum Green, where they have turned to the right across the Boldrewood Road, as if for Pugpits, but turned again to the right into the small fir plantation, where he was viewed across into Manor Park, and hounds ran very fast to the Mill again, then back to the Manor House, where he was headed by a man, and came straight back into the Mill-Pond Copse, where the Master whipped off at five o'clock. That is the way to keep hounds in exercise during bad weather, and sportsmen on foot saw a lot of sport. I hope to be able to send you more next week."

March 1886

"On Monday, 1st, with Major Browne, at Hythe Crossroads, we found in Cadlands, and killed after ringing about 10 minutes. Found another soon

Figure 8.3 "Now is the Winter of our Discontent"

The winter of 1886 made hunting all but impossible but the N.F.H. soldiered on under the supervision of Major Browne.

(Taken from an old print)

afterwards, and ran straight to Ipley Farm, where he turned and ran back to King's Hatt. Scent being very good, the little bitches went too fast for most of us, and I did not take the time as my watch was stopped, as they will stop when you are not certain what time you turned in the night before. One incident of the chase was when a grey horse carrying a lad deliberately laid down for a roll in the water — a nice cool day for a ducking. Mr Mills, also, had a good day on Saturday the 6th, Battramsley Cross, where there was a good field out. Found in a cover close by. Ran across Setley Brake, where he turned to the right and ran straight to Dilton Farm, where he turned again to the right, as if for Boldre Bridge, when, having lose a shoe, I left them, but here they had a good run afterwards.

"This week has been one of trial and sorrow again, but I hope soon to have more sport to record, as frost does not usually last long here."

February 1886

"Mr Mills's hounds met on Wednesday, 17th February, at Holmesley Station. Found at once in the open. Ran towards Burley, turned short to the left; ran a short distance by the south-western railway, turned to the right across the Bog away to Collingshill, up the road, then to the right across the fields through Stag Park, away through the woods, across the fields, through Mr Esdaile's covert to ground in the earths on the top of the Bog. Time, 45 minutes. Found another fox in Holmesley, but did very little with him. A third fox found in Wootton ran a ring back to Wootton, through Holmesley, along the road towards Burley, when there was a holloa on the Lawn, but I do not know if the hounds did anything more or not. On Saturday last this pack met at Moyles Court. The first covert drawn proved blank, but the second produced a fox, although hounds did very little with him. The second fox was run to ground at once, but he was dug out and broken up. They had a very sharp 20 minutes afterwards, but lost him at the end, scent being very indifferent.

"Major Browne was not out on Tuesday last, so Kennett hunted the hounds. Found at once in Shave Green Enclosure, and after making one ring round the covert went away very fast towards Cadnam Bog, by way of the fields. A long check occurred when close to the common, but Kennett cleverly hit off the line again, and after some pretty hunting over the rough ground we ran him into Cadnam Bog, where a fresh fox was quickly on the move. He went away from the east end of the Bog towards Paultons, the hounds close at him all the way over the open, and reaching the covert some little way in front of the field, who had to make a long round to avoid the Bog. On coming up with the pack we found them driving him about in fine style amongst the thick laurel bushes, and, in spite of his frequent short turns, he was at last driven out over the open heath again, where they killed him, Kennett alone being with them. He was a fine dog fox and ran for an hour and twenty minutes with hardly a check. The brush was given to Mrs Nunn. The hounds drew Paultons and Tatchbury Coverts, and although a fox was on foot, he was too far ahead for hounds to make much of him."

The above extracts are taken from *Horse and Hound Magazine* by "St. George".

In the New Forest

"As in the beginning so is the ending of the season best enjoyed in the Forest, when plough and pasture alike advance in cultivation, so even the keenest of the keen amongst our best friends care no longer to welcome hounds excepting puppies to walk, which now engross their whole attention, when thoughts turn on the Chase. Down here sport still flourishes and hither come all who wish to prolong the season. Once more the toughest and safest horses are chosen for extra duty, and well it was to engage stabling betimes, for now every stall is full and beds are at a premium. We old stagers who know how to get down comfortably have no trouble, so on the Wednesday before Easter we found ourselves snugly located at the Crown Hotel with our horses, so we could look on almost with complacency (but we feel for others' troubles) while less careful folks sought in vain for quarters in Lyndhurst and the surrounding villages. There is never much time to note changes on the first night, but we missed Pearce, and amused ourselves acquiring news as best we could. Sport has been good, and the deerhounds had capital runs on consecutive Mondays, ending with a kill each day, and Mr Mills had a great run on Wednesday, when the survivors saw the fox killed on foot, as their horses were done.

"On Saturday the sun was hot as summer when we started to meet Mr Mills's Foxhounds at Wilverley Post, so we set out early, and sauntered quietly along in pleasant company. They have had some good runs lately, and there was a large field to meet them. George Sears, with a mixed pack, drew round by Burley Rocks and across the road, where they chopped a fox, but soon found another on Wilverley Hill, which hounds ran through Ferny Nap and Rhinefields to Pound Hill, where they divided, and when brought together again, by Blackwater Bridge to Ferny Nap, they could not get on good terms with their fox, so drew Burley Old and New Enclosures, and found another that went away through Knightwood to Oakley, and up through Boldrewood, to ground in Pug Pits, where we saw them no more, for, while bending under a tree, with only room to get safely by creeping, the stupid little mare jumped over a hollybush as if it were a hurdle, bringing this poor bruised back in violent contact with a sturdy limb of oak, so once more knocked out of time, after lying still till wind was regained we did not find hounds again. That evening a youth, who trembled violently as though he had seen an apparition, handed in the following, evidently scribbled by the mysterious one, on the crown of his hat, but unsigned —

'April 24th. The run of the season. After marking third fox to ground in Pug Pits, went back to Oakley (800 acres). First a whimper, in a second a burst of music, very soon followed by a holloa from Frank (second whip), then a chorus as the hounds drove along to the north-west corner, at a pace, for Ridley Wood, then due north for Roe; still right-handed till the Broomie-road was reached through the corner of Slufter, over the Ringwood road, Pug setting his mask straight for Pug Pits, to ground after 50 minutes that caused more than one horse to say Peccavi.'

"This must have been a really good gallop, and, from all account, only the Hon. Francis Denison, Major Downman and a few others saw the finish.

"Sunday was a lovely day, almost like early summer, barring the east wind, which is still treacherous as ever. The floral decorations in the beautiful

Church, where Lady Londesborough and other Ladies had completed their labour of love late on Saturday, surpassed description. Macpherson sent masses of white flowers, which were arranged with rare taste."

April 1886

"After another long rest I must again take up my pen to record some good sport that we have enjoyed. On the morning of Tuesday, 18th, although the ground was still very hard, the sun had great power at ten o'clock, so Kennett (in the absence of Major Browne) decided to go to the meet at Hilltop Gate. There were still a few hard and slippery places on the sides of the hills, but elsewhere it was quite ridable. Only three of four sportsmen, including Mr Bennett, were there, but the Hon. Gerald Lascelles and Mons. Duplessis came up afterwards. Hounds first drew some of Lord Montague's coverts, and then went on to the Nodes, where we once more heard the merry chorus, so welcome after nearly a fortnight's silence. They ran the fox across the Bog and up the steep hillside and making a short turn he ran back for the Nodes; here they rattled him about in fine style for some time, and he eventually slipped away unseen with only five couples of hounds after him. These hounds gave him a rarc dusting across the Heath, and, making a short turn back, was met by the body of the pack coming up and killed. He was what 'Jorrocks' would call 'the biggest fox what ever was seen' and, although only a last year's fox, weighed quite twenty pound. His mask was almost black, and had much longer hair on it than is usual; the pads and brush were also peculiar, the former having hair all over the bottoms, instead of showing the bare feet. Some seem to fancy he was a cross with a collie dog, and his whole appearance might lead one to suppose that such was the case. We drew the open heath and patches of gorse, and the hounds marked a line all across the Common, but the fox was disturbed while running the other, so had too long a start of us. Having drawn the thick covert by Ipley River, the hounds were taken home. We are glad to hear that good sportsman, Major John Browne, has been presented with his portrait. He is represented standing, and looking down at a book on a table.

"On Saturday, 20th, we all took in a day with Mr Mills's Foxhounds, at Wilverley Lodge, where we had to wait half an hour on account of the fog. They found close to the Lodge, and hounds ran for twenty-five minutes to ground, so he was dug out and given to them. Later on they found a brace in Wootton, but they were home-rulers. That couldn't be induced to face the open. They found another fox in the open, and ran towards Burley, till they lost him, as there was not much scent. The fog was very thick in places, but better than frost any day."

April 1886

"On Friday, after a frosty night (quite a "blackthorn winter"), a large field met Mr Mills's Foxhounds at Ocknell Pond. Major Browne, with his two sons, rode out to see them, and Mr Bradburne, his successor was there too. In the absence of the Master, Mr Meyrick took the command and it was like old times to see him to the front on *Seagull*, for that boy on the white pony had not forgotten how to skim across the forest. With the lady pack, George Sears drew the gorse brakes on Ashley Plain, in search of a grey old varmint that has often led them a chase. The first fox, found near Hale, was left to her own devices, and hounds were taken to Islands Thorns, where they found at once, and ran through Alders Hill to Amberwood, across Driftway, to Sloden, and away over the open for the main earths, but being headed he turned back into Sloden, and ran a ring, again breaking away for the earths, so we gave him a scream or two, and with a whisk of his brush he set his mask straight for Broomie, with hounds racing him right through, away over the open; a glorious gallop to Slufter, through this, away to Pug Pits with never a chance to draw rein; right through and over the Boldrewood-road, through Holm Hill and Holliday Hill into Knightwood, where hounds divided, and a fresh fox was viewed into Viney Ridge, so hounds were stopped after a really good run of an hour and twenty-five minutes. Horses had enough of it, for the going was deep and the old stager again laughs at the success of his ruse.

"On Saturday, luckily, the weather was bright and more genial for the enjoyment of some thousands who assembled on Lyndhurst Racecourse to see the annual sports. Everyone who is anyone, and a great many who are not anybody in particular, were there, and spent a very pleasant day, without the slightest hitch in any of the arrangements. Lord Londesborough and Mr W.E. Bryan, the Hon. Secretary, were assisted by a strong committee, and all the events were well contested."

August 1886

"Saturday last was Mr Bradburne's opening morning, cubhunting with the Foxhounds at Furzey Lawn. It was like old times to set out early from the Crown Hotel; for in Mr Meyrick's day we have often been at the kennels before daylight, and seen good sport, getting home in time to rouse ordinary folks out of their beds. Four years ago, on July 29th, when the ground was hock deep, we had a memorable hunting run of three hours; and again, two years ago, on August 1st, we had capital sport on the first day, so we always start full of hope, even on such a day as this, hoping against hope, with all the enthusiasm of a sportsman, though a worse day for hunting could not be. Instead of a nice dew, there was hot, muggy air, with storm rain threatening, and everyone knows what that means, dry below and moist above — no scent 'atal, atal', but as we were able to hunt and see old friends, we must tell the tale and make every allowance for bad weather.

"When Major Browne gave up the Mastership at the end of last season, Mr Bradburne of Lyburn came forward, and, besides the hounds which he found in the kennel, has improved the pack by young drafts from others, and got together a nice little stud of hunters. Young John Dale, from the Croome, is huntsman, with Will Perkins first, and Allen from the Heythrop second, whipper-in. It was just five o'clock when hounds were thrown into covert in Brochis Hill Enclosure, and at a quarter past they found a cub, which soon crossed the road for the earths on the hill, and, finding them closed, took a turn down the bog, as if for the Manor, wither his sire had already gone with a few couples in pursuit till they were stopped and brought back. On the wet ground hounds could run a pretty little ring towards the kennels, round to Brochis Hill Enclosure, again lower down, and round again. One of those minor catastrophes that often occur in the Forest necessitated a temporary retirement for repairs. Luckily, the kennels were handy, and so on the *Gem*, only able to walk there, cantered gaily back, to find hounds still hunting in the

Figure 8.4 Good Hunting

(Taken from an old print)

Enclosure. With them were the Master and his son (unfortunately Mrs Bradburne, who is very fond of hunting is not yet well enough to go far from home so early in the morning), young Squire Compton of Minstead Manor, Mr Goldfinch, Mr Powell, Mr Weyland Powell, Mr Wingrove, Mr Bennett, Mr C. Downman, and Mr Merry from Bicester, besides several on foot. There was no chance to kill a cub when the ground got foiled, so a move was made to that covert between the kennels and the Manor which they call Haggis, one of the prettiest coverts in the Forest. Here are nice warm banks, facing south, thick undergrowth and a ready larder, everything that a fox could wish, so no wonder a litter was soon afoot— bright, ruddy little rascals, that whisk their little brushes when a halloa hastens them over a ride. At seven o'clock a brace broke across the Park for the Rhododenrons, with the pack running merrily over the grass; but in the Shrubberies scent vanished and with several foxes afoot, all was trouble till the Master wisely decided to take his hounds home, though sorely against his inclination to do so without blood on their first morning. Before these notes appear we hope to have an early morning in the Manor, and, with rain that has fallen scent might improve, so some of these little red rascals may cry — 'Capevi'.

"In the more open forest from Wilverley Post, Mr Mills's pack was luckier, for George Sear killed a fox above ground on Saturday, whereat was much rejoicing amongst those who were there: Lyndhurst is a gay little village, for the merry tourist always find plenty to do, and this morning, after breakfast, there was hardly time for the usual forty winks in that cool corner of the Crown Garden before going to bid farewell to the Volunteers, and watch them striking camp which was quickly performed with true military regularity. Luckily, there is not much history this week, for other affairs are so pressing. Goodness only knows how it can be done when the regular hunting season begins, for even now notes are jotted down at odd times under much difficulty, but, so long as readers are satisfied and stern critics lenient, you shall hear as often as possible from 'Dragon'."

23rd April, 1887

"Lyndhurst very full this season and last week when the Hunt Ball brought extra company together, there was neither bed nor stall unoccupied in the village after 4 in the morning.

"Lord Londesborough has been out every day, piloted by Mr Bryant.

"The Hunt Ball was one of the most brilliant and successful ever seen in the Forest. Everything was well done. The ballroom was beautifully decorated with ivy, and trophies of the chase, antlers and foxes masks and brushes. Flowers from Northerwood Park completed the effect. Everyone spoke highly of the supper and none of the 270 guests suffered from the Pommery Greno, 1880.

"On Friday Mr Bradburne's hounds met at Boltons Bench. It being hot, Lord Londesborough sent down a round table from Northerwood which was placed on the cricket ground and we all enjoyed an ice cool draught from a golden necked bottle, which was very refreshing on such a hot day. There was a very large field assembled after the Ball so the Master very kindly allowed a little extra law for latecomers while two photographers, Harvey and Short, took pictures of the scene. Dale and his whips looked smart and businesslike with 15 couples of mixed hounds. The weather was not much like fox hunting and we were agreeably surprised to see hounds able to run when they found a good fox in Matley Bog at 1.10. On good terms with him they crossed the railway into Deer Leap Enclosure and rattled him along the line nearly to the station, recrossed the line and raced to the Lyndhurst Road, where they checked after running 20 minutes.

"With eager horses before and behind them they had no chance but Dale cast them around Busketts and Ironshill and then back to Rifle Butts, but without hitting him off. So they drew Busketts and Fletchwood and back to Deer Leap where we viewed some very good stags but no fox. So we went on to Shave Green where a fox went away at 5.30 and away we went through the wilderness over the small fields and Akers Down into Pug Pits. Up and down that great Covert until hounds were whipped off at 6.15 with only a small percentage of the field left to tell the tale."

19th May, 1890

Talking about the crowds during April . . .

"However, there is plenty of room to ride when hounds have been running for half an hour, as in most other countries. It is easy enough to get horse boxes onto the South Western Railway from other lines. We chartered a horse box with double coupe and ran right through the whole show — three horses, a second horseman, all the luggage and a goodly luncheon basket. We were released at Lyndhurst Road Station (Ashurst) in the cool of the evening, just as the scarlet coated sportsmen were wending their way home after a good day from Boltons Bench, and the sight cheered the horses after their long journey, so that they trotted gaily along to the dear little forest village (Lyndhurst) and were soon in the old quarters at the Crown, and Harvey had, once more, room for a little one.

"After a stormy night with some frost and snow flurries during the early hours, Friday was a bright cool day when a large field met Mr Pierce's hounds at Stoney Cross at 12 o'clock. A gay field too, for besides a goodly array of New Forest scarlet and green collars, there were several uniforms of other hunts including the picturesque blue of the Goodwood. Povey found at once in The Grove but it was some time before he could get away. However, after several attempts he broke away over the open to Pug Pits. Locals call this a spinney, but it must be at least a thousand acres, and hounds were some time working through its deep recesses before the fox was viewed away back to The Grove, where, after some good hound work they killed their fox. Then drew Shave Green and found a good fox in the Hollies near Cadenham and ran through Shave Green to Brockis Hill away out to the Kennels on the right, they hunted beautifully to Faircrop, skirting Lyndhurst Racecourse, crossed the road and stream nearly to Ashurst Lodge where they swung right and quite a respectable little brook came into the line which claimed sundry victims. As hounds ran very fast by the Rifle Butts and we viewed the fox close up before them into the thick gorse near Boltons Bench. Here he laid up till they pushed him out over to the barn at Glass Hayes at the back of which they accounted for him after a run of one hour and fifteen minutes. Everyone was satisfied and Povey shall have his funny bone for a scarf pin as we have not seen a fox better hunted by hounds or huntsman anywhere this season.

"A small field met Mr Mills's foxhounds at Picket Post at 11.30 for the Forest was hard and dry so there was no scent. After a good season men, hounds and horses are very fit and no-one knows the run of the Forest foxes better than George Sears, for when they go to ground he remembers each one like a personal friend and knows where to look for him again. He has some female acquaintances too that he is not so pleased to meet at this time of the year so hunts with the circumspection that is not understood by all his followers!

"They drew Lord Normanton's coverts, High Wood, and another near Sommerly, then into Appleslade and Linwood, down Red Shoot Wood into Pinnick Wood where they found and ran up Handy Cross Plain, turned here short back into Roe and could make no more of it.

"The Hunt Ball was that night well attended as usual, and enjoyed by all. Mr Gerrard excelled himself in the decoration, the supper was very good and a thousand oysters went down in 40 minutes without a check!"

Saturday, 26th April, 1890

"Dull and cold without rain, just the day that we expect hounds to run in the Forest and nor were we disappointed, except that we allowed too little time to get to the meet. Mr Mills's hounds met at Marlpit Oak at 12 o'clock but George Sears had heard of a fox on his way there and was soon after him. So as we rode through Hinchlesea at 12.05 we saw hounds running along the opposite hill into Wilverly Enclosure and we had a stern chase after the vanishing pack. We soon found many of the immediate followers just as hopelessly lost. Finally caught up but the fox had won the day. Then drew Set Thorns and found a very good fox that led them a fast ring around the enclosures before going away over Mead End Common, round into Broadley, and back across Mead End Common, across the fields to Swaye, to a snug little gorse covert at the Hollies. Here he dwelt for we saw the remains of his supper last night — the feathers of a thrush and beneath them a dead worm on which the poor thrush had no doubt been too intent when he fell prey to the fox. And now that fox broke away in view of the field where, with hounds close at him across the fields to Mead End when he too, in turn, provided a meal for his relentless foes, to the good old tune of 'Tally Ho, Tally Ho! and Who-whoop', after a run of an hour and 20 minutes which satisfied everyone. So George took his hounds home at 3 o'clock on Primrose Day which will be marked in red letters in many hunting diaries. Concerning that little yellow flower which now signifies so much especially on this day, there were few coats and no habits undecorated. If dainty fingers were unavailable to fix them (we were particularly favoured in this respect), sportsmen who in the hurry of starting had forgotten, could supply their deficiencies from each bank or hedgerow as they rode along. The forgetful ones were easily spotted by their soiled boot soles!"

30th August, 1890

"Mr Pearce's hounds go out three days a week — sportsmen have plenty to do on non-hunting days, and there are always the studios to visit."

". . . in Woodfidley another was found at 8.10 and we viewed him across the ride near the railway. But his sire was handy and hounds settled onto the old stager out across the open to Denny, round to Woodfidley again, up to

Stubby and through Ramnor to Park Hill. Back across the driftway, through Ramnor to Park Hill. Back across the driftway, through Stubby once more and Woodfidley, crossing the railway line into New Copse and back again. The fox then took to the railway line and hounds were close behind when a train came along. It was a sight to make a man's heart stop, but the driver pulled up in time and hounds came out alive. Not one was injured. The number of the engine was 42 and you may be sure the driver will reap his reward. Povey took the hounds home and it was well for that old fox who lives with a run of 1 hour and 40 minutes to his credit."

The above extracts are taken from *Horse and Hound Magazine* by "Dragon".

9

The Second Mr Compton

1895–1905

Figure 9.1 Mr Henry Francis Compton, M.F.H.

Master of the New Forest Hunt from 1900-1905 and Chairman from 1927-1943.

Original painting being the property of Mr P.J.P. Green, the grandson of Mr Compton, with whose kind permission it is reproduced here.

(*Photo*: John Tarlton)

CHAPTER 9

The Second Mr Compton

1895–1905

Mr Henry Martin Powell of 'Brooklands', Lyndhurst, having amalgamated the country again, retained Povey as his huntsman. This Povey was a good huntsman, quiet with hounds and a consciencious worker. However, he had a morose and moody personality, and in a fit of depression, when the supply of foxes was in some doubt due to the great outbreak of mange in the late 'nineties, he poisoned himself at the cross-rides in Puckpits enclosure. He was replaced by Frank Hutchins who had previously been 1st whipper-in.

H.M. POWELL

Mr Powell's pack was comprised basically of those purchased by Mr Lascelles in '85; no strong hound policy had been adopted by the intervening Masters. Mr Powell was a great admirer of **Grafton** blood, as was his great ally Mr Henry Francis Compton — "The Squire" — and for some years the pack was increased by the **Grafton** draft as well as the home-bred puppies.

Mr Compton was a dashing horseman and owned a lovely black thoroughbred called *Black Satin*, Mr Compton called him *Satan*, which reason can be imagined!

This horse left everything standing when he ran in N.F.H. Point-to-Point members races in 1895, '96 and '97. In '98 he won again easily. However, it was found that he had gone the wrong side of a post and was disqualified. Indeed, everyone bar the last two riders had followed him, and those two — Admiral Murray and Mr Hesletine were the surprised first and second places that year. *Satan* gained sweet revenge the following year, however, by winning again with a handsome lead.

Mr Powell decided that the country could stand three days a week with the odd Bye-day thrown in, and with the invaluable support that he had from Mr Compton and Mr Lascelles, hunting was the best since Mr Meyrick's lamented resignation.

FOX AFFLICTION

Mr Powell hunted the bitch pack and Povey initially hunted the dog pack. Towards the end of 1895 the outbreak of mange among foxes which had been sweeping the United Kingdom for some three years, and indeed had stopped hunting altogether in many countries, reached the Forest. Gerald Lascelles writes, "Not only were dead foxes, horridly diseased, picked up all over the Forest, but in some cases we found badgers, woefully afflicted also, either dead or wandering about blind with disease, and that by broad daylight".

The Forest was more fortunate than elsewhere and the supply of foxes never failed, although the normally plentiful population was seriously depleted. However, by the time that Mr Powell handed over to Mr Heseltine (1899), things were improving again due to Mr Lascelles "rules", regarding digging — "After February 1st, all main earths which ought to have been stopped all the season, to be opened out, but all earths to be put-to on hunting mornings, very early. After 1st March, all stopping of earths in any way to be abandoned. After 1st April, no digging of foxes run to earth to be permitted".

YOUNG SUCCESSOR

Mr Christopher Heseltine of 'Walhampton Park', near Lymington, a tremendously keen young member, offered to take on the Mastership when Mr Powell decided to give up. His brother, Godfrey, carried the horn for the very short time that Christopher was Master, for upon the South African war being declared both hurriedly volunteered and left the country in December, 1899, when things were at their blackest and the nation was very alarmed at the situation.

The two "Heseltine boys", as they were known, had founded the Walhampton Basset pack in 1889 (now the **Westerby**), and had hunted with both the foxhounds and buckhounds almost since they could walk. Mr Godfrey Heseltine subsequently became Master of the **Walhampton** again from 1910 to 1915 and 1920 to 1932. He was also very successful as Master of the **Ootacamund Hunt** in India and, incidentally, introduced the New Forest green collar as part of the Hunt uniform. The hunt still survives, thanks mainly to his excellent work in "raising the establishment to the level of an English Hunt". His enthusiastic improvements to the country, making it more possible to ride over, it being heavily wooded and boggy, are still in use today, although the area is now a National Park and the **Ootacamund Hunt** followers are the only people allowed to hunt there.

The sad, terse comment in the N.F.H. records, against his name, informs us that he "committed suicide on August 5th, 1932".

Before he left for South Africa, Christopher had laid plans to carry the hunting on to the end of the season in a satisfactory manner: Mr Ernest Wingrove, the Hon. Sec., standing in as Acting Master with Frank Hutchins, 1st whipper-in, hunting hounds.

These arrangements were very temporary however, and at the end of the season, in April 1900, the Hunt found itself once again without a ready successor to the Mastership, although with the largest subscription list ever, before or since.

Figure 9.2 A Young Master

At the age of twenty-eight Henry Compton took on the Mastership. He is pictured here in a painting by John Emms, 1893, with his Beagles. 'Minstead Manor' can be seen in the background.

(*Courtesy*: P.J.P. Green. *Photo*: John Tarlton)

HELP FROM "THE MANOR"

Once again the Compton family stepped into the breach — in the form of Henry Francis Compton who offered to hunt the country, as indeed his great grandfather, John Compton, had done exactly 100 years earlier. The guarantee of £1,500, not a great deal of money even then, was agreed and the Hunt enjoyed five years of good settled management under this popular Master. He was renowned nationally as a good judge of hounds and in fact travelled the Kingdom judging at hound shows, such as Peterborough.

He particularly favoured the **Dulverton** and **Grafton** blood, and made much use of the **Dulverton** line stemming from the **Badminton** *Rustic*, a Peterborough champion, who combined good looks and excellent working qualities. At the Peterborough Show in 'Coronation Year' 1902, he was delighted to see his "chosen" bitch, the **Grafton** *Rakish* carry off first prize, and Mr Cazenove who accompanied him there declared that he spoke of little else for days.

Whilst he was Master he hunted the bitch pack and his kennel-huntsman, J. Jones, hunted the dog pack on alternate days, three days a week. He was only twenty-eight years old when he took on the Mastership, and he combined his duties with that of J.P., Deputy Lieutenant for Hampshire, and being a leading member of the Conservative Party.

ADMIRAL MURRAY

In 1901 a tragedy occurred on a glorious September cubhunting morning. Admiral Murray, a popular member of long standing was thrown from his horse on Backley Plain whilst hounds were being put in to the first draw. He died instantly of a broken neck and hunting was abandoned and hounds sent home. A subscription was taken up from his many friends in both packs and this was used to make a passage across the bog from near Pound Gate, Puckpits, across to Lucas' Castle. It was marked by a small stone, still there today, which though weatherbeaten is readable, and of course this eminently useful track is known as "Admiral Murray's Passage".

The Admiral, who was sixty-nine, had had a remarkable career, serving as mate on the *Arethusa* during the Crimea, and had commanded the *Agincourt* during the Egyptian campaign of 1862. Only two seasons earlier he had caused a great commotion at a meet at Boldrewood. Arriving at the meet in great style, driving tandem, his horses bolted as he was handing over the reins to his groom. He was thrown clear and escaped with a dislocated arm. This clearly gave him pause for thought and, being the methodical naval gentleman that he was, he actually made all the arrangements in advance for his own funeral. He even purchased a tombstone, inscribed with all the details of his naval career, and a plot in Ringwood Cemetary.

MR COMPTON'S RESIGNATION

In 1905 Mr Compton, feeling that he was not able to devote sufficient time to his domestic affairs, handed over the Mastership to Mr Powell again. He remained, however, as a leading member in the Hunt, and a great figure in Forest life. He was Chairman of the Hunt Club for fifteen years, from 1928 until shortly before he died in 1943.

Also in 1905 there was a change of Chairman. Since 1886 Lord Montague of 'Beaulieu' had been a practical and strong Hunt Chairman. Upon his death in 1905, Sir George Meyrick, who had been Master from 1878-85, assumed the position of Chairman and remained until his death in 1927, bringing with him that same enthusiasm and love of foxhunting that had marked the golden years of his Mastership.

It is worth noting that although Lord Montague's son was a noted sportsman with hound and gun, he astounded friends and neighbours alike in being interested in engineering matters to a remarkable degree. Particularly in that new fangled phenomena, the motor car. Indeed he founded the magazine *Car* and he was the first member to use a car to get to meets. He gave up riding to hounds in 1910, resigning his membership in 1912 — in those days it was customary to resign membership of the Hunt Club unless one rode and/or paid a full subscription.

HUNTING DIARY 1895-1905

18th April, 1895

"Wednesday 10th April; met at Vinney Ridge. A pleasant sunny day and we found almost at once in Knightwood Enclosure but hounds could make little of it, scent being poor and their fox having dodged about a good deal. However, after a time they hit off a line in Mark Ash which they hunted prettily up over the hill and away through the hollies and beech trees for a little while. Then drew Holmhill; then onto Soldiers Bog and a disheartening long draw. But perseverance was at length rewarded by Maurice hallooing a fox from the hills above Pinnick at 5.20. When Mr Thursby got to it, hounds simply raced down to Roe, through it, out the other side at the lower end up into Red Shoot, through to Appleslade and so on at the same pace to Moyles Court when alas the fox had gone to ground above the road and near the new buildings. Only 12 minutes but one of the fastest 12 minutes that ever was seen! After which they went home."

Taken from *Horse and Hound Magazine* by "St. George".

1895

"These hounds had their opening meet at Boltons Bench on Tuesday October 22nd, but the weather was so wretchedly cold and wet, that they had but a poor day. Although they found twice they could not run a yard.

"On the 24th they met at Ashley Lodge. After the two days rain the ground was in good order and the weather was bright and sunny, there being a very hard frost in the night. On account of illness of the Master, who I regret to say will not be out for some days, Povey was hunting the bitch pack. There seemed to be no lack of foxes in this part and unfortunately one got up in the midst of them just above Ashley, and they chopped him. Found again on the hill but the scent was very poor and they could only walk after him round the hill and up to Ashley Wood where they lost.

"Later on at 2 o'clock they found in Sloden Enclosure and after this one we had a pretty little hunt through the enclosure and away on a right hand circle towards Hasley and back up the outside of Alderhill. Then on a circle around the hills to the top of Amberwood. Up to this point the scent had been better, and it was delightful to see how hounds had worked on the line over the hills. They continued through Amberwood only being just able to walk after their fox, down to Sloden driftway, where Povey had to give it up, scent having absolutely failed. A pleasant day's hunting, and no lack of foxes, only scent was catchy."

Taken from *Horse and Hound Magazine* by "T.F.B.".

April 1899

"Larger and larger grow the fields here as one pack after another finishes the season and lets loose in habitual followers — that is to say, the keenest of the keen amongst them who will not be denied the pleasure of prolonging the best of all seasons to its utmost limit, and here this year we are having a real good time. There is not much to record on Thursday with the Deerhounds, for it was a most unlucky day. A nice warm morning and very large field met at the Ravens, where Mr and Mrs H. Martin Powell entertained us all. The pack was moved to Clay Hill, and there we waited till after four o'clock while the tufters ran deer in Park Hill. When a single buck was viewed across the road near New Park, it was more than an hour before the pack could be laid on, so they only hunted slowly to Hurst Hill and Queen's Bower. Then Mr Kelly gave orders to draw Fletchers Thorns with the pack, and when they found some deer they ran fast through Pound Hill to Vinney Ridge, where a leash were viewed, so hounds were stopped and taken home.

"After a rough, stormy night, Friday was a soaking wet day, with wind due east, which is always good for scent here. At the Hunt meeting, held in the Crown Hotel, everyone was glad to hear that Mr Christopher Heseltine has been appointed Master, with a guaranteed subscription and poultry fund, and we are also pleased to record that Mr H. Martin Powell showed us two clinking good runs on his last day as M.F.H. In spite of the wet, cold day a large field assembled at Bolton's Bench. No sooner were hounds in Little Holm Hill than a holloa towards Denny at 12.45, set us galloping, and after one turn round the great enclosure, they broke away towards Lyndhurst, and we had to gallop our hardest as they ran between Park Hill and Jones's Enclosures, crossing the road, down through Whitley Wood to Hurst Hill and skirting New Park, kept to the open, leaving Pond Heath on the right, into Rhinefield and Clumber, out over the stream, and across the rough Markway Hill to Wilverley, where an open earth close to Wilverley Post brought this fast run to an end after forty-five minutes. Mr Powell then drew Burley Rocks down to Burley New, and here they found again near Hobart's Cottage, racing through Oakley, out by Old House, across Backley Plain, crossing the Ringwood road near Handy Cross Pond, down nearly to Pinnick's Wood, but turned left-handed and recrossed the Ringwood road down to Ridley Wood. Through this they ran very hard to Burley Fields, where they threw up after twenty-five minutes and made no more of it. It is not advisable to ride the fields at this time of year, so the Master cast them round into the Forest, but to no purpose, and as every horse had now had enough, and every rider, male or female, must have been nearly wet through, it was well to turn homewards. It was a day of grief and disaster, so some were wetter and dirtier than others. There was one rare chance for the young and gallant foresters to distinguish themselves when one of their prettiest maidens was thrown in a bog, and with true maidenly modesty fastened her patent skirt before attempting to get out, which proved a sore handicap, and a young, gallant forester might not have been so irate as a brother, kept waiting with the captured steed. 'Tally Ho' will be really grieved to know that the geranium coloured gabardine coat that he so much admired is now nearly black, and we are going to hang it in our institute as a relic of what coats become in the Forest.

'How do you amuse yourselves on non-hunting days?' is often asked. Well, there have not been many so far. One day we drive to Lymington to eat prawns, and another to Beaulieu to eat oysters. We have noted the excellence of Lymington prawns before, but to us the oyster-beds at Beaulieu came new, so we wrote to Mr Selfe, of the Montague Arms, in time for a supply to be drawn from those beds and they were good. Our little people like boating now, for the captain of the ferryboat at Lymington took us all for a cruise across the river and back. A halfpenny a passenger each way and he told us he makes nine bob a day with each boat, so there is some profit attached to

Figure 9.3 Cubhunting Meet at Boldrewood

(*Courtesy*: Sutton's of Brockenhurst, *photo*: Brian Manby)

amphibious speculations. Mr Badcock has some old brown sherry left, and his parrot is loyal as ever. We always have a good time here."

April 1899

"On Tuesday, another large field met the Foxhounds at Boldrewood. A hot day, that brought the flies out hungry, so we were glad to keep moving. Hounds ran a short line to a big earth near Bushey Bratley, then drew Slufter and Ocknell Wood, where they found, and raced across the open to King's Garn, down this, and across to a new enclosure that we have not seen before, but it must be Salisbury Trench, up hill to the plain again, and over the open down into Syburn. Here some posts and rails caused disaster. Colonel Smythe had an ugly fall, and one or two others also, as hounds ran down to Hamptworth, where they threw up after a fast gallop of thirty minutes. Mr Powell held them on, but did not hit him off again. Drew Bramshaw Wood, Paulton's, Caddenham Bog, the Sir John Barleycorn,[1] and, as our illustrious chief knows, we found a good straight pint here, which came in more than useful. Then drew Shave Green, and trotted on to Minstead Manor, where of course they found in the famous rhododendrons, but a lucky view saved a valuable life, and we went home, after stopping to talk to the "Squire" about a dog.

"The Hunt Ball that night was a great success, as usual, and next morning shoe-horns were in demand for hats, so we were lucky to be in our normal condition. A very large field met the Foxhounds at Ocknell Arch on a wet, stormy morning. Foxes are not so plentiful in the Forest as they were when first we hunted here, and it is sad to see such long draws as we do now. When we read 'Porcupine's'[2] touching farewell last week we should have invited him down with his family, to enjoy themselves as we do, but he is a foxhunter pure and simple, and after the Cottesmore, if he found himself in a comparatively foxless forest, his sarcasms would probably burn holes in the paper. Well, Mr Powell drew Ocknell Wood and Slufter, then Broomey, outside which hounds showed a line just enough to excite a racing pony which had been requisitioned to carry a young visitor to the ball (everything on four or even two legs has to go these days), and the pony carried a passenger across to Milkam, and jumped at the iron hoop fence, over which the passenger went in safety, but the pony fell back and had to be shot. We missed all this, for hounds ran just well enough to be interesting till they lost their fox near Slufters. Then they had a very long draw, and we left them at 4.30 near Pug Pits. Here they found, and had a short gallop to ground before they all came home."

1901

"On Tuesday April 23rd another hot day. A large field met at the Manor when the Squire's round table on the lawn was more popular than ever. The Master was having a holiday while Frank Hutchins hunted and soon found a fox in the Manor that broke away for the Wilderness over Akers Down to Holm Hill where he beat them — a fast 20 minutes. By then it really was too hot to gallop about any more so went home. Master wrote 'The hottest day I ever was out in my life'."

The above are taken from *Horse and Hound Magazine* by "Dragon".

4th May, 1901

"Met at Boltons Bench with quite a large and fashionable attendance on horseback, foot and wheels, not a few of whom were on bicycles to welcome Mr Compton when he trotted up with his pack in the pink of condition which does the greatest credit to the Master and kennel-huntsman. I never saw them look anything like so well. Found in Matley Bog and ran over Ashurst Lodge back to Beaulieu Road Station where we lost the fox. Found again in Deerleap and ran very fast over Blackdown into Denny where we lost him after a very pretty hour's run.

Taken from *Horse and Hound* Magazine by "Red Hat".

15th April, 1905

Notice

Due to the retirement of the Master of the New Forest Hounds, James Jones requires a place as Huntsman, 1st Whip or kennel-huntsman. He has been with the N.F.H. 3 seasons hunting the bitch pack and previously was with the South Staffordshire. He has also hunted hounds abroad.

This advertisement appeared in the classified columns of the *Horse and Hound Magazine.*

1 A well-known local hostel.
2 "Porcupine", hunting correspondent of *Horse and Hound*.

NEW FOREST HUNT POEMS 2

CROWN AND STIRRUP

(New Forest Foxhounds)

See Note No:

At cover late, I heard, the other morn,
The bitches running, and the doubling horn.
They've found! "Hike Holloa!" Will has seen him break!
Some loiter; some reflect which line he'll take,
But ride, you boys, who wish to see him die!
The pack race to it, settle down, and fly.
Ride like the devil, else it's all in vain,
You might as well go straight back home again.

How are the mighty fallen! Put to rest
By forty minutes of the very best!
Let's see who now the striving pack can view.
Not many — those that can, good men and true.
First Harry Powell, in his place, of course, (1)
Well carried by that stout old whalebone horse.
And close to him his trusty henchman Frank (2)
(For that he has his good black mare to thank).
Pulteney and Matcham, though they both wear "specs", (3/4)
Riding as if each had a brace of necks.
Compton from Minstead, on his second nag, (5)
From find to finish I know he'll never flag,
Wingrove, the Sec., who's worth his weight in gold — (6)
Would that these sportsmen never could grow old!
Mount them alike on hunter or on hack,
By hook or crook they will keep near the pack.
There's Turpin hustling on his gallant grey; (7)
"Morny" and Lascelles, Tuck, too, on the bay; (8/9/10)
Brown on his new quad; Timson, Heseltine — (11/12/13)
These are the boys who with the pack can shine.

Dallas we miss; and I'll bet 10 to 1 (14)
In former days he used to see the fun.
The Colonel's sure to turn up at the finish — (15)
Yes, never will his love of sport diminish.
We seek in vain the old Doctor's cheery face. (16)
The fox in his beat held the foremost place.
Alas! to happier hunting grounds he's gone.
But "forrard!" lads; the pack keep driving on—
"Forrard! Hark Forrard!" See! from scent to view
The bitches racing — "Tally Ho! Leu! Leu!"
"Who Whoop! they've got him! Who Whoop! of earthly things
Hunting's the king of sports, and sport of Kings!"
Who Whoop!

(Written by Colonel Alec E. Cowie (late R.E.), January 1897, Member 1901-11)

A HUNTING PAGEANT

Preface

Milton and Chaucer both are dead and gone,
The classic Avon mourns the departed "Swan".
Why regret these? When Matcham still remains (4)
To sing of hunting o'er New Forest plains.

At Bramble Hill there dwells a bard,
His hat is flat, his name is Matcham,
He reels off verses by the yard;
I can't think how his brain can hatch 'em.

R.W.B., 19th April, 1898 (17)

NEW FOREST HOUNDS

I HENRY MARTIN POWELL, M.F.H.

With careworn face, lean form, and haggard eye,
The Master of the Foxhounds first rides by;
Sadly his thoughts o'er many subjects range
From poultry bills to owners, keepers, mange —
As through his troubled mind wierd visions stray.
Gloomy forebodings of the next blank day —
A wretched scapegoat on whose head is piled
A heavy load of criticism wild —
If scent is bad, meets wide, and horses lame,
Or foxes scarce; tis he alone to blame,
And after reddest of red letter days,
He gets the scantiest medium of praise.
What wonder then he shuns the babbling crowd,
Its ceaseless chatter, and its laughter loud,
And with a heart, heavy and cold as stone,
Surrounded by his hounds, jogs on alone;
Finding, when gloom and wrath his bosom fill,
A never failing safety valve in "Will."
But every cloud, we're told, bright silver lines,
Behind the darkness that the sun still shines,
As you may note, if you are standing near,
When "Frank's" shrill holloa strikes upon his ear, (2)
How instantly transformed our Master seems,
How with fresh life and joy his visage beams,
Spurring his willing horse; swift as the wind
He leaves his sorrows, and his cares behind.
Pleasure and hope his fears and troubles calm,
His echoing horn chaunts a thanksgiving psalm;
Then as he hears from many deep-toned throats
Come pealing forth the gladsome opening notes,
And as he sits and marks with kindling eye
The distant hounds as to the horn they fly.
And sees the pack go streaming o'er the plain,
Then Henry Powell is himself again.

II WILLIAM MARTIN POWELL

'Tis with awe and deep humility I take my pen to write,
I feel guilty of audacity infernal,
Choosing for the subject of the lines I now indite
The Father of the Hunt, the gallant Colonel.
When an urchin I was told "the boy is father to the man,"
But nowadays we travel so much faster,
And in this case seem to hit on quite a different plan
For the Colonel is the father of the "Master."
When he's hunting it's notorious, he "hangs a splendid boot,"
And of elegance, and ease, gives the impression;
None so qualified as he, to teach the young idea to shoot
Or "hunt" would be the more correct expression.
Horses, saddlery and "turn out" he'll severely criticise,
But the things that most annoy him, and are hateful in his eyes,
Are a snaffle, and a bridle decked with buckles.
Who so deeply versed as he is, in the many varied ills
That horseflesh (more's the pity) is the heir to.
There is not a vet (their treatment as a rule is "cures or kills")
Who can give him any points, that I will swear to.
He knows every inch of country, and the run of every fox;
And his usual hunting lunch consists in picking
(I apologise most humbly if the rhyme I'm making shocks)
The drumstick of a pheasant or a chicken.
Now I hope and trust sincerely, before my story ends,
That for years to come the Colonel may be seen
When not hunting, criticising all the horses of his friends
From his old familiar station on "Goose Green"

Figure 9.4 William Martin Powell

III HON. GERALD LASCELLES

And now let "Ave Caesar" be our cry,
Although I trust we're not "about to die,"
We must salute the Forest's uncrowned King,
And, raising high our voices, his praises sing.
'Tis but the duty of the humble Vassals
And tenants of the mighty Gerald Lascelles,
Despotic Ruler, Autocrat Supreme,
Whose word to question none would ever dream;
Though in these democratic days, it's true,
He has been bearded by a brazen few,
A sect who love contentions, squabbles, fights,
Stiffnecked, and stubborn as the Israelites.
Upon their sacred rights he dares encroach,
And is to them a "hissing and reproach".
The while they rave, and clamour, and abuse;
Their frenzy he with calm indifference views;
Though as a blazing fire their fury flares,
Like Gallio, for such things he nothing cares —
A many counselled man he might have been,
Such an Archbishop as we've seldom seen;
How well his manly figure would adorn
The Apron, and the snowy sleeves of Lawn;
He might have been an Admiral of the Fleet
Or on the woolsack proudly ta'en his seat;
Or had his thoughts towards war, and bloodshed turned
Doubtless a Marshal's Baton he'd have earned;
He might have been a great Prime Minister
With schemes like Machiavelli, deep and sinister.
Too great the task, for him, a choice to make
Among so many, which road he would take,
On which to sit, among so many stools;
Kismet decided — over as he rules —
A shrewd, experienced judge of Horse and Hound
A better sportsman nowhere can be found.
Or Falconry, by all the world it's known
As an authority he stands alone
Profound his knowledge both of beasts and men,
He owns the ready writer's facile pen;
Possesses ready wit and winning smile,
A voice that from the tree a bird could wile.
A tongue that could persuade one wrong was right,
That light was darkness, or that black was white.
None can its charm and eloquence resist,
He's also "something of a naturalist".

IV ERNEST L. WINGROVE

Here comes a face (a portly form it crowns)
Never disfigured by ill-humoured frowns;
That cheerful still, no matter what befall,
Ever benevolently beams on all.
Sur 'tis our "Sec." whose jovial, hearty air
Will from the gloomiest bosom banish care;
Peace and content wher'er he goes he'll bring,
And always seems as happy as a king;
And never, I am sure, has he been heard

To speak an angry or unkind word.
With cheery laugh, and heart quite free from guile
He greets us all with broad expansive smile,
For once "The right man is in the right place".
He at Hunt meetings often may be seen
Calling attention to the Rule Fourteen.
Urbane, and courteous: ever suave and mild
One "draw" there is whereby he may be riled,
When of his stewardship called to give account
And asked to name the "Funds" exact amount,
No one, as he, when e'er he gets the chance,
So energetic in the mazy dance;
But though a great admirer of beauty
He ne'er lets pleasure interfere with duty;
And with his honeyed tongue and easy tact
Contrives from all subscriptions to extract.
So well he's known, 'tis needless here to state
His horse, like his opinion, carries weight.
Long may he flourish, for 'tis very plain
"We ne'er shall look upon his like again."

V JOHN PULTENEY

You can talk of the bravest of heroes
From Richard the First down to Ney,
They would make a poor show across country
With Pulteney to show them the way.
How pale they would grow, and still paler,
Beginning to funk, and to shirk

Figure 9.5 Ernest L. Wingrove

If they had to play follow-my-leader
When he sat down to cut out the work;
And how they'd be picked up in pieces,
Broken collar-bones, legs, arms and necks,
The result of their trying to follow
The mild-mannered man in the specs.
He regards neither danger, nor distance;
There is no one so fearless and keen,
Be the pace what it will, or the country;
Wherever the hounds go he's seen.
The miles he has ridden, the places
He's jumped, I'm afraid to relate.
If one fence more than all his soul loveth
It's a strongly-made, high and locked gate.
I am certain his deepest affliction;
Worse even than laming his horse,
Is if hounds come to draw at St Austin's
And there isn' a fox in the gorse.
Without doubt his idea of a heaven,
Bands, halos, harps, wings — and all that,
Is jumping forever large fences
On the tireless ghost of old "Pat";
And lest ceaseless saltation in safety
At length peradventure might pall,
He'd prefer as a chance and excitement
To take now and then a bad fall.

VI HENRY F. COMPTON

Oh! Young Lochinvar he came out of the West,
And in all the wide border his steed was the best;
Without crabbing the horse of the Young Lochinvar
I will bet Compton's "Satan" is better by far. (18)
When the "Socman of Minestead" is well on the ride
There isn't another can live by his side,
For "Satan" has still got to learn how to fall
And his master rides paces like A. Nightingall.
When the time for our Point-to-Point races come round
At the finish the pair well in front will be found,
While the rest struggle home in a woe-begone tail,
Clacey leads back the winner once more to scale.
Harry Compton's the boy for diversion and fun
With beagles, or terriers, with rifle or gun;
But the sport next his heart is with horse and with hound
And a fox at the Manor can always be found.
He is cheery and friendly and courteous to all,
He'll ride hard to hounds, or dance hard to a ball.
That he's quite our "show man" we all freely confess,
And we'll hope that his shadow may never grow less.
He's a chairman, a "beak" and a Verderer too,
His friends they are many, his enemies few;
I believe he has all that a man can desire,
So here's luck and long life to the young Minstead Squire.

VII COL. EDWARD PALK

Who next appears? Upon the well-bred grey,
Beaming on all, with jest and laughter gay;

Always brimful of merry quip and talk —
You need not ask — of course it's "Piggy Palk," (19)
Quick witted, cheerful, who so fond as he
Of risque talk, bon mot, and repartee?
A boon companion, full of chaff and banter,
His favourite pace, a Rotten Row-like canter,
But we must leave him, and his merry laugh;
Here in a dog-cart comes his better half,
No need has she of clumsy motor car,
For "Blacky" in the shafts is better far.
Keen her enjoyment of all sport and fun,
Of every fox she seems to know the run.
Judgment and instinct, both must have a share,
For at the finish she is always there.
It has been whispered that some sportsmen say
"Oh! What a second horseman thrown away."

VIII R.W. BLATHWAYT

B stands for Blathwayt, bold and bad, (17)
Of wrath a most capacious vessel
Who never strives ('tis very sad)
With mankind's enemy to wrestle.
With gold-rimmed specs, and aspect mild,
He might pass for some harmless Curate,
But Oh! his language when he's riled,
I'm sure that you could not endure it.
It's not so much the things he'll say
(His repertoire is poor and scanty),

Figure 9.6 Henry F. Compton

But said in his most vicious way,
They'd terrify a wild Ashantee.
There's nothing can his love efface
For sport in every form and fashion;
The wild New Forest Deer to chase,
His great, his chief, his ruling passion.

IX CAPTAIN RICHARD TURPIN

'Tis of Captain Richard Turpin I am now about to sing,
A task that I perform with greatest pleasure;
Though I fear I can't describe him as "an artless little thing,"
I may safely call him "quite a perfect treasure".
He is fond of wit and humour, has "a most engaging way",
Takes no part in petty squabbles, fights or quarrels,
And the only thing about him I regret that I must say
Is "His manners are much better than his morals."
So courteous, mild and affable, so gentle he appears,
I feel sure he ne'er would give you the impression
That a man of war and bloodshed he has been in former years,
And to fight for Queen and country, his profession.
He dearly loves a story, and he dearly loves the chase,
He's in our New Forest Hunt a great believer,
And the runs as he describes them, both for distance and for pace,
Put to shame the Quorn, the Pytchley and the Belvoir.
Now old "Roderick's" but a memory, he rides a gallant grey
(When it meets a German bad it's rather tricky);
He's a shining light in Lyndhurst, where we hope he'll always stay
For we never could get on without our "Dicky."

X FINALE

In the New Forest wide, there are so many ride
That the names of them all I can't mention,
As was, I may say, when commencing this lay,
My original plan and intention,
I have said what was true of each man that I knew,
Un-biassed by fear or affection,
And now that 'tis done I must hope there's not one
Who objects to this morale dissection.
If there's ought that offends that I've said of my friends,
Great my sorrow, and deep my remorse is,
Though I cannot but fear, some will say with a sneer,
"His rhymes are as lame as his horses."
As I must be exact, I shall just state the fact
That we, as a Hunt, are not "dressy,"
But as all the world knows, out of place are fine clothes
In a country so muddy and messy.
There are ladies galore, always well to the fore,
A goodly and gracious procession,
But bolder than I would the man be who'd try
To mention them all in succession.
Always right in the front, at the top of the Hunt,
Jack Powell to go is a "one-er," (20)
And no marvel, for he is a gunner.
And another brave man, always well in the van,
So slim, and so smart, and clean shaven,
Heseltine you will note, in an up-to-date coat, (21)

**And, by jove! he's no funker or craven.
Brother "Chris" by his side, always ready to ride,** (13)
**No one fonder than he of a flutter;
Through the hairiest place, with a grin on his face,
He goes, as a knife goes through butter.
Splashing round like a frog, there is "Hope" in a bog,
Big and black, more or less as it chances,
For sometimes, we know, he can't choose, but must go
Wherever his wayward horse fancies.
You will find any day, in the thick of the fray,
Reynolds, Forman and Gambier hustling.** (22/23)
**At a deuce of a pace, as if riding a race,
May see Admiral Murray go bustling,** (24)
**Always cheery and keen, in the front he is seen;
Of a Hunt Challenge Cup he's the holder,
And if truth must be told, while we're all growing old
The Admiral grows younger, not older.
Then the way "Downman" goes is what nobody knows,** (25)
**For ten to one "on" is the betting;
When we're all beat and done at the end of a run
He'll appear with his horse still curvetting.
There is yet one more pair, who will surely be there,
Regard not banks, timber or water,
No matter their size, they've no fears, in the eyes
Of "Clowes" and his brave little daughter.** (26)
"Bradford", too, you may spy, always ready to buy (27)
**Our screws, or sell one to a client.
With the hounds any week you have not far to seek
Ere you come on the sport-loving "Bryant."
You will find not a few representatives too
Of the Forces who guard and defend us
By land or by sea or wherever they be,
All riding with keenness tremendous.
And a great many more, but I told you before,
And I do so again, though with sorrow,
If I mentioned each one, I should never have done
Though I wrote until this time tomorrow.
The first wish of my heart till I have to depart,
And extinguished are life's dying embers,
Is "Luck and good sport of the very best sort
To The New Forest Hunt and its members."**

Written by G.E.E. Eyre Matcham, c.1900.

SOURCE NOTES TO POEMS

1 H.M. Powell of 'Wilverley Park', Master 1894-99, 1905-07. Member of the Hunt for fifty-three years and reunited the country 1895. Died 25th November, 1943.

2 Frank Hutchins, 1st Whip and kennel-huntsman to Mr H.M. Powell.

3 Mr Keppel Pulteney of 'Northerwood Park' and St. Austin's, Lymington. A member for fifty-two years. Died 8th December, 1944.

4 G.E.E. Eyre Matcham of 'New House'. A member for forty-one years. Died 10th July, 1939. Writer of *"The New Forest Hounds"*.

5 H.F. Compton of 'Minstead Manor', Master 1900-05. Member for fifty-one years and Chairman from 1928 to 1943. Died 15th April, 1943.

6 Ernest L. Wingrove of 'The Oaks', Ashurst, Lyndhurst, Hon. Secretary 1887-1932. Member for fifty-eight years. Chairman of Committee and Field Master 1916-18. Died 1941.

7 Captain Richard Turpin, a sportsman who lived in a cottage outside Lyndhurst on the Beaulieu Road.
8 Mornington Cannon, one of the most famous jockeys of his day. A regular follower and subscriber to the New Forest Hunt.
9 Hon. Gerald Lascelles, C.B., third son of 4th Earl of Harewood, Deputy Surveyor of the New Forest 1880-1915. A great supporter of all sport and excellent administrator. Hon. Member 1880. Born 1849, died 1928.
10 "Tuck", a sporting farmer from near Christchurch, well known in his day.
11 Probably C. Berney Brown of Sway, Lymington. A member 1891-99 and keen supporter.
12 Major H.T. Timson of 'Tachbury Mount', Master 1914–15.
13 Lieut-Colonel Christopher Heseltine, O.B.E., of 'Walhampton Park' and afterwards of 'Brambridge Park'. Master 1899-1900. A member for fifty-three years. Died 13th June, 1944.
14 Charles Dallas of Eastley, Wooton. Died 1955. Member from 1885.
15 Lieut-Colonel William Martin Powell of 'Brooklands', 1824-1909. Hon. Secretary 1853-87.
16 Probably Doctor R.G. Freeland of Brockenhurst. A member for twenty-nine years. Died 27th September, 1943. Dr Freeland was not on the telephone and continued to drive round to his patients in a dog cart.
17 R.W. Blathwayt of Boldre. Born 1850, succeeded to 'Dyrham Park', Gloucestershire.
18 *Black Satin* Henry Compton's well known horse. Otherwise known as *Satan*.
19 Colonel Hon. Edward Arthur Palk of 'Little Testwood', Totton. Born 1854, 4th son of 1st Baron Haldon.
20 Brig-General Edward Weyland M. Powell, C.B., C.M.G., D.S.O., of 'Brooklands'. M.F.H., United, 1910-19, Meath 1919-22. Born 1869.
21 Major Godfrey Heseltine, Master of Ootamacund Hounds and Walhampton Basset Hounds. Born 1871, died 1932.
22 Jack Forman of 'Setley House', and 'New Park'. Died 1900.
23 M. Gambier of 'Buskett's Corner'. Member, 1896-1921.
24 Admiral Murray of Poulner, Ringwood. Member 1895. Killed hunting 1901. A memorial bridge erected to his memory in Withybed Bottom, near Lucas Castle, south of Stoney Cross.
25 C.B. Downman, a permanent member for fifty-three years. Died 1939.
26 Colonel Clowes of 'Bartley Close', Totton. Member 1897-99.
27 Bradford, a well-known horse dealer at Brockenhurst.

10

The Edwardian Afternoon

1905–1918

Figure 10.1 Mr Walter De Pradine Casenove, M.F.H.

Master of the New Forest Hunt from 1907-1911.

(*Courtesy*: Sutton's of Brockenhurst, *photo*: Brian Manby)

CHAPTER 10

The Edwardian Afternoon

(1905–1918)

Mr Henry Martin Powell's second term of office was altogether a happier time for him than the troubled and anxious years of the 'nineties, when he had had the sudden death of his huntsman and the blight on the fox population to contend with. His dashing style of riding ensured the large fields of the day, including many visitors, and he pleased the purists too, and was described as "the best woodland huntsman who ever lived in the Forest".

VISITORS

The Forest continued to attract visitors to its unique hunting area. Brockenhurst and Lyndhurst were full of small guest houses catering for the needs of visiting hunting people. Of course 'The Crown' at Lyndhurst was always first choice, but when the old 'Grand', opened just before the turn of the century, they too catered almost exclusively for sportsmen.

Every sporting magazine gave space to writers such as "Dragon" to write about this "unspoilt tract of country". All larded heavily with warnings on how to avoid the infamous bogs!

After two years Mr Powell decided to hand over the Mastership and was awarded that enviable honour of being elected a permanent member.

MR W.D.P. CAZENOVE

The new Master was Mr Walter De Pradine Cazenove of 'Langley Manor', Totton. Jones, who was originally Mr Compton's huntsman, was now hunting hounds for Mr Cazenove, and although it was remarked that he was not "as quick as his predecessor", he showed good sport and accounted for a remarkable number of foxes during his Mastership.

He was not a Forest man by birth, having come via such Hunts as the **Wilton** and the **Woodland Pytchley,** at both of which he held the office of Master. However, he often said that he was a New Forest man by adoption, and that like all converts he was more fierce in his faith than those who grew up to accept it!

MR COOKE-HURLE

When he retired after five seasons, Mr John Cooke-Hurle undertook to hunt the country jointly with his brother Major E.F. Cooke-Hurle. Prior to coming to the Forest Mr John Cooke-Hurle had hunted the **Lamerton Hounds** in Devon from 1904 until 1910. Both men rode well and competed each year in the Point-to-Points. In 1913 Mr J.A. Cooke-Hurle took 1st place in the heavyweights, on his best hunter *Lamerton* but Major Cook-Hurle took only second place to M.K. Pulteney on his *Golden Grove* in the lightweights. In the previous year the races were run in the most diabolical conditions as heavy frost had frozen the light snow that had fallen overnight. The results were as follows:

Heavyweights:	**5 starters**	**1 finished**	**Rest fell**
Lightweights:	**6 starters**	**4 finished**	**Rest fell**
Farmers Race:	**5 starters**	**5 finished**	
Tradesman's Race:	**4 starters**	**2 finished**	**Rest fell**
Open Race:	**8 starters**	**2 finished**	**Rest fell**

Still they were wonderful hunting years; this period afterwards being known as the "Edwardian Afternoon". The Empire was at its zenith, there was peace; it was **fashionable** to be wealthy and to enjoy it.

A CHANGING WORLD

That great friend to hunting in the Forest, Gerald Lascelles retired and with him, almost, went the end of an era. He wrote, shortly afterwards in 1915, "Whatever may be in store for sport and for old England as the outcome of the terrible times in which I write, is on the knees of the Gods. But of this I feel sure, that, as the earliest recorded hunting began in the New Forest nearly nine hundred years ago, and as the Forest itself was formed in the first instance for the sport itself, so it will be the last of our English countries in which the sport of hunting will come to that end which we all trust is very far off". For as he left, the world was changing and would never be the same again. Mr John Cooke-Hurle had already resigned in late 1913 leaving Major Cooke-Hurle as sole Master. However, in 1914 he received advance warning that he also was to be ordered to the Front. The following notice appeared in the annual subscription lists for 1914.

"Owing to the outbreak of the European War which necessitated the resignation of Colonel Cooke-Hurle, in consequence of his military duties, the Committee appointed by the Members of the New Forest Hunt Club arranged with Major Timson at the end of August, 1914, to carry on the hunting of the country until the end of the season, 1914-15. The total expenses of hunting the country throughout the season 1914-15, including the amount paid to Colonel Cooke-Hurle, and also all sums paid for repairs to the N.F. Hunt Kennels, amounted to the sum of £1,545 7s 3d., whilst, in addition, the sum of £241 15s 6d was expended in satisfying Poultry Claims*. The New Forest Hunt Club Fund has accordingly had to be drawn upon to defray the deficit."

Written by Ernest L. Wingrove, Hon. Sec. New Forest Hunt Club.

"T.T."

Major Tommy Timson, therefore, served in double harness with Major

*Poultry Claims Fund: paid to farmers who, in preserving foxes for The Hunt, had lost poultry to raiding foxes. This payment has now been discontinued in The New Forest but is still carried out in some other counties.

Figure 10.2 The New Forest Hounds in Kennels, 1912

(*Courtesy*: The New Forest Hunt Club)

Cooke-Hurle until the latter was posted, and thereafter hunted the country with the aid of a committee consisting of Sir George Meyrick, (Chairman); Ernest Wingrove, (Hon. Sec. and Field Master); Captain Compton, and Messrs. Jeffreys, Martin Powell, Thursby and Downman.

Major Timson had some years earlier been the Master of the buckhounds for a short time, the only person to achieve this "double", and incidentally he was the grandson of the Rev. E. Timson who had been Master of the N.F.H. in 1854.

In 1914 he was stationed at Romsey and was considered by his contemporaries there as "an amusing character, who was a past master, at what one might call, getting away with it". As so often happens in wartime, discipline was far stricter at home than overseas and the Romsey Depot was rather overweighted with this factor. For a season and a half, however, "T.T.", as he was known, used to slip away to the Forest, stopping en route at 'The Vine' at Ower to change into hunting kit, before putting in an appearance with the hounds. After hunting he simply reversed the process— even to the extent of arranging a hot bath to be kept waiting for him, and returned to the camp for evening stables. As hunting had been reduced to two days a week and he had a "neat little sporty car" this presented him with no real difficulty, and he kept up the scheme until he was discovered, and sternly advised to change his arrangements. Shortly afterwards he was transferred to Swaythling Remount Depot, and was unable to hunt hounds. However, even here he got a 'name' for himself by his love of practical jokes.

Swaythling was then on the extreme borders of the **Hursley** and **Hambledon** countries. One evening at dinner he let slip that hounds might be in the big woods behind the depot the following day.

Next day after mid-day stables as the officers were returning to the mess for lunch, a horn was heard in the woods at some distance. Without further ado **every** officer vanished at a gallop in the direction of the horn. Only one or two spotted the deception when they saw "T.T." galloping like fury across a ride, horn in hand!

THE WAR YEARS

However, to get back to the Forest, where the committee was putting up a grand fight of it. To begin with, all decent horses, that is anything that looked like it might be able to raise a gallop, were requisitioned by the army. Some were, however, excused on grounds of age, or for necessary agricultural work.

Food for both hounds and horses was extremely short, but Mr Wingrove as Acting Master, together with the committee, managed somehow and although the hunt staff, horses and field were composed entirely of 'veterans' over military age and ladies, hunting continued during those terrible years of the Great War.

A great help was Mr O.T. Price of 'Ironshill', a previous Master of the buckhounds and a strong supporter of the N.F.H. He placed his terriers at the disposal of the Hunt and these played a great part in not allowing the fox population to get out of hand in the country during those years. Lord Lonsdale, M.F.H. of the **Cottesmore**, made a present of a few couple of bitches to the Hunt.

One of these bitches bred a litter of five extraordinarily good workers; the three dogs were *General, Gambler* and *Gainsborough*. *Gambler* in turn sired a stallion hound *Warrior* who left his mark upon the kennel. *General* was quite a character by all accounts and would not leave a 'dig' even when the rest of the pack was taken on to another draw. He meant to have his fox!

When he grew older he was so highly regarded as a worker that "O.T." used to take him to the meet in his car — and home again at the end of the day. Fred Cooper was huntsman at the time, and although he had the added problems of wire, the new aerodromes, experimental bombings and practise ranges, no one would deny that he did a grand job.

Many young members who went off to fight never returned and the Hunt rolls are scattered with the comments "killed in action in the Great War"; records meticulously kept by Mr Ernest Wingrove.

At first the committee, like many other hunts, had considered temporarily disbanding the hounds for the duration. But there was an outcry from the young men going abroad, and an impassioned plea from an 'old stager', who pointed out that there were many old hunters who would be wasted, foxes would get out of control and many grooms and servants, not to mention merchants, who would, perforce, be flung out of work if hunting did not continue.

In 1914 they were still hunting four days a week but by 1918 they were down to two days a week. The Secretary's seasons report for May 1918 was as follows:

"Scent was very fair and it was quite an average season. Hounds killed 17½ brace of foxes in 54 days on which they were out. None of them being blank. Owing to the number of keepers from the district that are serving their country, great difficulty was experienced in getting the earths stopped and consequently many foxes were run to ground. The best day was Saturday, 8th December, 1917 when the pack met at Forest Lodge, Hinton. Finding a fox in Harrow, hounds forced him away over Poors Common, past Thorney Hill across the railway by Whitten Pond to Burley and thence to Burley New Enclosure and Dameslough to ground in Knightwood. A point of seven miles. Joe Overington the whipper-in has now left us to take a similar position with the Quorn."

11

Sir George Meyrick

1919–1956

Figure 11.1 Sir George L. Meyrick, M.F.H.

Master of the New Forest Hunt from 1919-1952.

(*Courtesy*: Sir George Meyrick, *photo*: John Tarlton)

CHAPTER 11

Sir George Meyrick

(1919–1956)

In 1919, with the end of the Great War, a new Mastership began. It was that of Major George Meyrick, later to become Sir George; and it was destined to last for a record thirty-seven years.

MEMBERS OF LONG STANDING

There are, incredibly, still members hunting today who hunted with him in those early days — Mrs Pat DuPré and Miss Rachel Pulteney for example, both of whom started riding to the New Forest Hounds as children in 1919 and only gave up recently after nearly sixty years! They both still hunt regularly on foot however, and there are many others who remember those 'old days', and speak of them with great affection and nostalgia.

For a couple of seasons prior to the War the Major had carried the horn at the **Ootacamund Hunt** in India and, of course, he had hunted throughout his childhood in the Forest with both packs.

He returned from the fighting, as did most young officers, with a fierce determination to keep, at all costs, the England that they knew and loved. For the Major, foxhunting in the 'old style' was his way of preserving the lifestyle for which he had fought.

OLD FASHIONED STANDARDS

C.R. Acton, who wrote *Sport & Sportsmen in the New Forest* in the early years of Sir George's Mastership said of him, "Here we have an example, and one of the last in England, of a country Squire, brought up to the old fashioned standards, who is making a brave fight to keep the flag of Foxhunting flying, in the old fashioned way. In the early days of his Mastership, Major Meyrick lived at Lyndhurst, and seldom was it that a non-hunting day passed without his walking down to the kennels. People were only slowly settling down to their occupations in this post-war period, forest fields were small and, for the most part, consisted of keen foxhunters — and they had a keen Master.

"I treasure memories of those days concluding on the twilight uplands above Boldrewood, the dark masses of Oakley Enclosure below us, already seeming inpenetrable in the gloaming, or on the top of Hampton Ridge, with the vast expanse of the sweeping open Forest, mysterious in the sunset afterglow; and then with 'Goodnights' said, hounds would turn away for their long trek home in the dark. The Master's pipe— that sure beacon of the close of a hunting day, in full blast, epitomising, somehow, relaxation after a long and tiring outing."

Figure 11.2 A Lady Rider

Major George Meyrick (later Sir George) and his wife, Mrs Meyrick, at a meet at North Gate. It was not until 1914 that women began to form a large proportion of the field.

THE NEW ERA

The main differences that the men returning home from Europe found were wire and ladies. The wire was mainly in the outlying cultivated areas, but in those days hounds hunted a much larger area than now. The River Test and the Southampton Water marking the eastern boundary with the Solent marking the southern boundary as far as Lymington; the Avon at Ringwood pretty well forming a natural western boundary as far as Downton in the north across to Whiteparish and Awbridge. Rachel Pulteney remembers one of her favourite hunts over Pepperbox Hill, overlooking Salisbury!

Of course ladies had hunted the Forest since at least 1802 and possibly even before that. But from 1914-1918 they represented over 70% of the field. Such hunters as had not been requisitioned, were at the disposal of the wives and daughters who hunted and schooled them, almost as a matter of duty, against the return of their menfolk. Ladies became more skilled at riding difficult and strong horses, whereas before the war they rode only well mannered horses. Then of course riding astride became socially acceptable and this seemed to many a more sensible way to ride in the trappy Forest country, and *de rigeur* for those who, without grooms, now 'did' their own horses.

Other changes were the marked decrease in the numbers of farmers riding to hounds and, for no really explainable reason, an improvement in the general standard of horsemanship and the condition of hunters.

Mr George Whitehead, the Hunt's oldest member, is now in his eighties and alas, no longer able to hunt. He was made a member of the Hunt Club in January 1923 and, as I write, he has been a member for more than fifty-six years; he hunted in the Forest prior to the 1914-18 war. He recalls that when they first returned from the war they were not able to do more than two days a week. On Tuesday's they hunted in the centre of the Forest — around Lyndhurst — and on alternate Saturdays they hunted the north, Fritham and Hale, or the south, Burley, Brockenhurst and the surrounding area.

There were few meets even then, in the cultivated farmlands of the south, although hounds did meet as far out as 'St Austins'; the Pulteney family home at Boldre. They had two whippers-in, so were able to hunt with about twenty couples of hounds, a great help in drawing the big enclosures. The small fields greatly appreciated the fact that the Major was most considerate about blowing his horn and **never** left them standing. On winter Saturdays he would always go on drawing as long as there was light, even on the most cold and unpromising days.

RABIES OUTBREAK

In 1919 there was a severe outbreak of rabies in the U.K., said to have been introduced by dogs smuggled back by soldiers. All dogs had to be muzzled and to be led when in the open. Special exemption was given for the hounds; but they forgot to ask for one for the Hunt terrier, so he had to go and live in the lodge with the hounds. A small hole was cut in the kennel door, so that if things became too lively inside, the terrier could get out, but the hounds couldn't!

In 1923 there was a large and important meet to celebrate the 36th year of

Mr Wingrove's Secretaryship, which he had augmented by also serving as Acting Master, and Field Master for some years. They met at 'Cadlands', the family home of the Drummonds, and the field of 120 was the largest since pre-war days. A dinner that night at 'The Crown', Lyndhurst, was held in order to present him with a piece of plate bought by subscription; in fact he was destined to go on for a further nine years, finally resigning in 1932.

DEATH OF THE CHAIRMAN

The fields gradually grew, from forty to sixty to eighty riders. In 1927, following the death of Sir George Meyrick, the Major succeeded to the title, and moved from 'Ballard Lodge', Lyndhurst, to the family seat at 'Hinton Admiral'. The death of his father was indeed a sad blow to the New Forest Hounds, for he had long been a leading supporter. It will be recalled that his brilliant Mastership in the 'seventies and 'eighties of the previous century had been one of the bright lamps in the Hunt's history.

He had become Chairman in 1905 and had continued in this office for twenty-two years, steering the Hunt through the difficult war years and into the financially perilous 'twenties. It need hardly be said that during these years he had heavily subsidised hounds. Upon his death Mr Henry Francis Compton, ex-M.F.H., was elected to the office of Chairman.

From 1928 hounds hunted on three days a week; on Thursdays they hunted that wild 'remote' northern part of the Forest. Fields were smaller because of the inaccessibility, but just as today the best sport was seen there.

DOLLY

A famous local character, in those days, was *Dolly*, a small bay Forest pony. She pulled a governess cart around the Forest on hunting days, carrying Mrs O.T. Price, the wife of a leading member, and the hunt terriers— each terrier housed in a separate little canvas bag. *Dolly* was always there when needed, for she was able to use tracks and rides that motor cars could not hope to tackle. It has often seemed strange to me that more followers today, especially those who have given up riding, do not take to this method of following. Mrs Price also carried in the cart her famous ginger-whisky, a "life restorer on cold days".

Sir George's kennel-huntsman then was Jack Candy, a much beloved man in the Forest who lived for his hounds. "Me little playmates", he called them at exercise.

He was with Sir George from the start and hunted the dog pack on alternate days. Another well known face on the Forest scene was Fred Day, ex-Master of the beagles; since his resignation he had bred and kept the Hunt terriers, along with "O.T." and was never missing from a day's hunting. He lost his life in a peculiar sort of hunting accident. He loved nothing more than 'a dig', and one day whilst digging out a large badger set at the end of a hunt, a thorn penetrated the skin of his arm. He thought no more about it and within days he was dead from tetanus.

There were four lawn meets a year at 'Hinton', and at that time this included an automatic invitation to breakfast. All the farmers in the New Forest country were also invited on these occasions, and the Master firmly

Figure 11.3 Jack Candy

The kennel-huntsman leading hounds to a meet at 'Stockley Cottage', January 1920.

(*Courtesy*: Sutton's of Brockenhurst, *photo*: Brian Manby)

upheld that old tradition of keepers' and earthstoppers' feast. A tradition which, I am happy to say, has recently been revived.

The Hunt Point-to-Points were held at Nea Croft, near Bransgore, on a property belonging to the Master. It was a small course but well laid out. The Point-to-Point Secretary was Major Tinker, of Chewton Glen, and he made sure everything was "exactly right". Most of the gentlemen who were good riders entered — either in the heavyweight or the lightweight races.

SECRETARY FOR FORTY–FIVE YEARS

In 1932 that marvellous man who had been Honorary Secretary for forty-five years, resigned. Mr Ernest Wingrove had first taken on the office from William Martin Powell in 1887. He had twice stepped in and acted as Acting Master and Field Master during war periods. Mr George Ferguson of Coppithorn Hill, Copythorne, then took over this important task.

In the late 'twenties and early 'thirties the depression hit hard, and the foxhunting community suffered as badly as anyone. Sir George waived the guarantee and hunted hounds at his own expense for more than four years. As the stormy financial situation settled and fields began to swell again, Sir George became a noted judge of hounds. He was still insistent upon hunting in the Forest being carried out in a manner which was to be of the highest standard.

That old tradition of spring hunting in the Forest returned in part, and many visitors came each April from those countries where hunting had finished for the season. Strings of hunters were trundled down by train, and all the big houses and local hostelries bulged at the seams. Hunting five days a week with the two packs, and large and fashionable parties were the order of the day, and it was onto this gay and glamorous scene that the storm clouds of World War II started their ominous rumblings.

WORLD WAR II

One of the first to go was the Honorary Secretary, George Ferguson, serving as Lieutenant Commander R.N.V.R. He was to lose his life in *The Prince of Wales* in December 1941. The role of Hon. Sec. was then taken on by Major P.P. Curtis: "Toby" to his friends.

Toby had grown up in the Forest and was now living at Bank near Lyndhurst. He had hunted throughout his childhood, was a first-class horseman and had come back to hunt there whenever his military career had allowed. In World War I he had served as a Brigade Major and G.S.O. II in very heavy fighting. Later, he was well known as a top steeplechase jockey.

Hunting continued during the war, with much the same sort of deprivations and problems that the previous one had brought. At least there was no horse requisitioning to contend with.

Hunting was immediately reduced to two days, and after autumn, 1942, was further reduced to one day. The main problems encountered were the crop of aerodromes at Stoney Cross, 'Beaulieu' and Holmsley; barbed wire and camps; trenches; craters from the low level bombing practise runs; not least the new rides, deeply cut, and drainage foiled by the haulage of the timber so desperately needed for the War Effort.

Figure 11.4 A Man and his Hounds

Jack Candy with his "little playmates" pictured here talking to Mrs Pulteney, c. 1924. His death in 1942 was a severe blow to all who knew him.

(*Courtesy*: Miss Rachel Pulteney)

Most of the members were either away fighting, or involved in the War Effort in some way. The veterans who were not called away served locally in the Home Guard. These were the ones who kept things going; those serving could always rely on squeezing in a hunt in the south of the country when home on a precious leave. It kept them going! The north of the Forest, around Ashley, was cordonned off as a restricted area, but the area around Lyndhurst, Brockenhurst and Rhinefield still gave them an enjoyable hunt in the very darkest days.

DEATH OF JACK CANDY

In 1942 Jack Candy died suddenly of pneumonia, to the immense regret of everyone who knew him. It was a severe blow to Sir George. Fortunately Fred Perry, retired huntsman of the **Albrighton** was living at Bank and came forward to take Jack Candy's place. At the end of the war, his son Ralph Perry became kennel-huntsman, with Fred whipping-in.

PICKING UP THE PIECES

After the war, hunting on two days a week was resumed. The war debris was removed fairly quickly, but, of course, the fixtures — the aerodromes and trenches— remained, and the new network of roads was responsible for one of the greatest face changes in the Forest's history.

Before the war there were no roads in the Forest, other than at Rhinefield and the Ornamental, and these were gravel tracks. There were only the 'trunk roads' to the West on which trundled the odd car. Sir George used to swear furiously at any motorist whisking by at more than 30 m.p.h. Now of course there is a positive lacework of roads and tracks throughout the entire Forest.

Fields were very small, frequently numbering only a dozen, whilst people tried to recover and pull some sense of order into their lives. Side saddles, whilst seen occasionally, were definitely the exception, rather than the norm.

LADY MEMBERS

In 1947 a major change to the Hunt Club rule was carried. It stated that henceforward lady members would be admitted. The ladies, however, were not thrilled at all by this storming of the hitherto male bastion. Indeed, they refused in droves to have their names put forward. Most had grown up accepting the Club as a purely masculine affair, and had no desire to intrude. Consequently, although two or three ladies were elected each year it was well into the middle 'fifties before the leading ladies in the hunt would allow their names to go forward.

Prior to this rule change, ladies who were the wives or daughters of a member had been allowed to wear the Hunt Button, upon the Masters' invitation, although not, of course, the collar. Rachel Pulteney clearly recalled the thrill when on returning from hunting her father gravely informed her that the Master had said she might now wear the Hunt Button. She was seventeen at the time and enormously proud of the privilege of being allowed to sport the coveted button.

THE HUNT BALL

The ladies of course have always played a large part in organising the Hunt Balls; at least since World War I. These were much more 'glamorous' affairs than now, presided over by the lady patronesses. In order to get a ticket one had to be 'vouched for' by one of the ladies and, Hunt Club member or not, if the ladies didn't approve, you didn't get a ticket!

After the war the Hunt Balls were held at 'Morant Hall' in Brockenhurst. This building is no longer in existence but even then it was showing signs of its advanced age. The ladies of the committee used to denude every tree for miles around of its ivy in order to literally cover the walls and gallery of the ballroom; decorating in the Hunt colours of scarlet and green.

Dress was extremely formal, and even after the World War II some of the older ladies wore 'court' feathers in their hair. All ladies wore the long 'fourteen button' gloves and, of course, their grandest ballgown.

It was considered infra dig. to arrive at the ballroom before 10 p.m. In fact, most of the crowds started to drift in from their pre-ball dinner parties around midnight, suitably primed for the gaiety. A large orchestra played all night and dancing went on until dawn. A cold supper/breakfast table was laid in a separate room, where one retired to eat around 3 a.m.

There was a gallery around the ballroom and Arthur Rickman, the present Hunt Club Chairman, nostalgically recalls standing in this looking down on the brilliantly colourful scene, as dancers whirled around the floor, in the days when people 'danced' and the majority of gentlemen wore scarlet evening dress.

Incidentally, the reason for the New Forest Hunt Ball being held in April dates back to the days when spring hunting in the Forest drew fashionable crowds from all over the Kingdom.

THE 'FIFTIES

By 1950 things were looking better; people were beginning to come out hunting again, although even by today's standards fields were small, numbering thirty or forty and most of these being staunch followers for many years. Among them were a group of ladies who were 'the first flight'. Mrs Susan Green (the Master's daughter), Miss Rachel Pulteney, Miss Priscilla Hunt and Mrs Marriot comprised a formidable spearhead and many of the gentlemen who hunted then tell me that "no man could live with them on a stiff run, for they knew the Forest like the back of their hands, and they rode like fury". The sturdy five-bar gates into the enclosures were scorned by them on a run, when the pace was too good to stop and unfasten them. I am told though, that there was "a hell of a row if you broke one!".

In 1951 Ralph Perry left to go to the **Croome**, and Frank Peachy came in as kennel-huntsman, having previously served in Essex.

By the middle 'fifties, Sir George was suffering badly from severe arthritic pain. This stemmed, mainly, from a badly set leg which had been broken in the early 'thirties in a hunting accident over at Burley Rocks.

Days became much shorter and fields became smaller. It must have been a most difficult thing for the Master after thirty-seven years to make the final decision to resign. Even at the end he always saw his hounds fed after a

Figure 11.5 A "Victorian"

Sir George at a meet at Brockenhurst Bridge. His fine mastership helped to carry the Hunt through the turbulent war years.

hunting day. He never believed in motorised transport for hounds — they hacked to all meets, so this feeding routine was sometimes very late after a long hunting day.

SIR GEORGE RETIRES

In 1956 he finally resigned as Master, remaining as Chairman of the Hunt Club. Toby Curtis, who was also feeling the years he had put in as Honorary Secretary, resigned at the same time. Really it was the end of an age. Sir George, who has been described to me as "Victorian", had run the hunt in an almost autocratic manner; maintaining the old high standards in the field and on social occasions.

The Hunt was indeed lucky to have this stable period of management to take it through the turbulent years of two world wars and a major depression.

Many are the stories of Sir George but the one I like best was told to me by Mrs Jane Boyce, who hardly ever misses a day's hunting even though she hacks to all meets.

It seems that the Master was a director of the old Southern Railway, and there was a 'halt' on this line, at his property, at 'Hinton Admiral'. Sir George had always enjoyed the privilege of having a train stop whenever he required to take him up to town. Shortly after the war when the company was pulling in its horns, the Board wrote to Sir George to inform him with the deepest regret that they could no longer afford to make these unscheduled stops. The Master totally ignored this impertinent missive and the next time he was going to town rang the office to tell them to meet him. Astonished, they politely reminded him of their letter and he, equally politely, but one may assume somewhat icily, advised them that he would be waiting. He was — in a chair parked plumb in the middle of the track! Of course the train stopped and Sir George got on. I gather that there was no further nonsense experienced from the Railway Company.

HUNTING DIARY 1919-1956

15th January, 1925

"This day would be hard to beat. The Master was hunting hounds and there were two good runs. This first was for an hour and ended when the fox managed to slip into a convenient earth; the second was a hunt of two hours and hounds killed in the open in front of the Royal Oak, the same fox they started on for Jack Candy identified him. Besides the Master there were only Lady Meyrick, Jack Candy and three others up at the end."

Taken from *Horse and Hound Magazine* by "Sydney the Standard".

February 1931

"Found in Blacksmith's Bog, and ran by Bramshaw Wood, Lyburn, Longcross Pond, Linwood, Malwood, The Bentleys, Holm Hill, Milkham, Roe Wood, Pinnick to Marrow Bowls Hill where they lost. They covered some 20 miles as hounds ran with a furthest point of 9½ miles."

1933

"Another fox found in the same bog as above was run into in the grounds of Ironshill Lodge, the home of O.T. Price, in a hunt of 1 hour 50 minutes, with a point of 6½ miles."

1934

"A very good run during cubhunting gave a good gallop when a fox found at Ipley ran over Beaulieu Heath, Norle, Pylewell and they lost their fox in Pylewell Park within sight of the Solent. A point of 7½ miles."

The above are taken from *Sports & Sportsmen in the New Forest* by C.R. Acton.

1935

"Found in New Park, ran to Rhinefield, Oatfield, through Wilverly Enclosure and Holmsley to ground in Cuckoo Hill. This was a 10 mile point and probably over 20 as hounds ran."

February 1936

"From the Bisterne meet the Foxhounds did not do very much in the morning, but had a good hunt late in the day from Thorny Hill, out to Avon Tyrrell and the Ripley lane, where the fox turned back— probably headed— and hounds were stopped on reaching Bisterne Common again. From the Barley Covert, Cadnam, hounds had a good day with two good hunts. The first fox was killed in the open in the Cutwalk, after an hour's run, and the second was marked to ground in some thick rhododendrons near Brown's Cottage.

"The Brockenhurst Bridge meet heralded a very heavy day of ringing hunting, the furthest point from Brockenhurst being Burley New. Hounds were eventually stopped in Rhinefield Sandies. The bitches killed a brace on this Saturday, and marked a third to ground, and were hunting continuously all day. One of the foxes was chopped, and, of course, the deed took place in New Park! Just to emphasise how odd these New Park foxes are I will describe the chop in detail. Mr O.T. Price was out in his car on this occasion; he was walking, with his terriers, in the covert near New Park Farm. Suddenly they made a dive towards the undergrowth and put up a fox. Mr Price went out into the field and halloaed; he watched the fox out of sight, apparently making for the top covert that borders on Hurst Hill. He halloaed for four minutes, and hounds came. They picked up the line at the exact spot where he last saw the fox, and brought him back, in view, the other side of the hedge by which he had run, had what Will Perkins described as "a fast burst of two minutes," and killed him. Will Perkins, by the way, is a fine old Forest veteran, he used to be whipper-in to the Buckhounds under Mr Lovell, of Hinchelsea, and the way he gets about on foot still is wonderful. Now, that fox must have been sitting in the ditch, in spite of the halloaing; why on earth did he not go on to the covert, where he must have known that there were fresh foxes? This chopping complex of New Park foxes quite defeats me. The place has been cubhunted more than once, and a brace were killed there the very first morning.

"Talking of quaint 'fox' situations, recently in the Forest hounds had marked and Mr Price rode off for his terrier. He returned, immaculate in his scarlet coat and topper, but with the terrier under his arm and a couple of spades slung round his neck. 'Oh, for a camera!' said someone. However, the terrier was put in and the dig took place. At the psychological second Mr

Figure 11.6 The Opening Meet

Sir George Meyrick at Boltons Bench, Lyndhurst c. 1931.

Price called out to the Master and stood aside for the fox to bolt. Hounds dashed in too soon, knocked Mr Price into the trench, and broke their fox up on top of him. 'Master!' yelled Jack Candy, 'pull out Mr Price, Pull out Mr Price!' And all that could be seen of him were his pathetically waving boots. 'Oh, for a camera,' indeed! But all's well that ends well; they got the pack off quickly, and neither he nor his terrier was hurt."

Taken from *Horse and Hound Magazine* by "Sydney the Standard".

12

Bringing the History Up-to-Date

1956–1980

Figure 12.1 Sir Newton Rycroft, M.F.H.

Seen here hunting hounds in the North of the Forest, 1964.

(*Photo courtesy*: Jim Meads)

CHAPTER 12

Bringing the History Up-to-Date

(1956–1980)

THE COMMITTEE

After Sir George's resignation it was decided to run the Hunt by committee for a season or two, in order to assess the situation before advertising for a new Master. For the last fifteen years, at least, everything had been managed entirely by Sir George and Toby Curtis, so that no-one knew how things really stood, or how to go about running the country.

Therefore, with Mrs Pat DuPré taking on the role of Honorary Secretary, a committee was formed of the following members:

Colonel Geoffrey East (Chairman of the committee)

Ralph Hill	John Morant	Mr & Mrs Faire
L.C. Martin	Mrs Rayner	Major & Mrs Dunlop
Sir Gervaise Tennyson	Squadron Leader Vernon Simmons	

The main problem that they encountered was undoubtedly one of an appalling financial situation. Sir George had, during the entire period of his Mastership, heavily subsidised the guarantee, and so there were no reserves in hand, nor were there any fund-raising activities in hand, as none had previously been necessary. Today these fund raising functions serve two purposes: they assist in supporting the ever increasing costs of keeping hounds and, just as important, they enrich country life. I am referring to hunter trials, gymkhanas, country fairs, horse shows, terrier racing etc.

Due to Sir George's failing health, hunting had fallen off in the last years of his Mastership, and fields were correspondingly small. One of the first things the new committee had to work at was increasing this subscription list to create immediate revenue. Frank Peachey remained as huntsman with Peter Smith turning hounds to him.

To encourage new and young subscribers, hunting days were longer. Hounds were now boxed to outlying parts of the country, so that they were able to go on drawing much later. The mere fact that these outlying areas were being hunted again meant that new people were reached, and it was also at this time that subscribers from a much wider section of the community were attracted. As Arthur Rickman put it, people ". . . from outside the foxhunting classes!".

THE SUPPORTERS' CLUB

Ralph Hill formed the **Supporters' Club** in 1957, "principally to create an

Figure 12.2 Frank Peachey (huntsman) hacking hounds on to a draw near Burley, 1960.

(*Photo courtesy*: Jim Meads)

interest and deeper involvement in hunting for foot followers, and to encourage new support". Slowly the required amount of finance was acquired to run the hunt for the year; and then another year. However, it was touch and go at times, and Pat DuPré often thought that they would not survive another month.

A TRIUMVIRATE OF MASTERS

In 1958 it was decided to advertise for a Master for the forthcoming season. There were some replies, but no-one was thought suitable. Then Mrs Cynthia Darling, who lived locally, wrote to Sir George, who was then Chairman of the Hunt Club, and suggested that she would be prepared to take hounds on if a suitable Joint Master could be found. Sir George, therefore, asked Colonel East if he would take on a Joint Mastership. It must be accepted that, in considering this, any potential Master had to take into account the amount of finance he, or she, was going to have to come up with at the end of the year to make good the deficit from subscription revenue.

Anyway Colonel East accepted, provided Ralph Hill would also come in as Joint Master, which was exactly what happened and the triumvirate were gratefully accepted. Sir George was always there in the background to help whenever approached, but he never interfered, a remarkable thing when one considers his close involvement during the previous years.

In the event, Mrs Darling only remained for one season and so Geoffrey East and Ralph Hill ran the country together for the next four years; a most difficult period whilst the hunt learned to stand on its own financial feet.

Geoffrey East had been hunting with the N.F.H. since the late 'twenties when he met Sir George out hunting with the **Pytchley**, and had been invited to visit. He came down with his two good hunters, both "super jumpers", and meeting the lady of his choice, found that one of the horses exactly suited her. So that was that! He remained in the Forest, married and the couple made their home in Bartley, oddly enough, next door to Mr Gilbert's old house at 'Lambs Corner'.

GHOSTLY INCIDENT

Colonel East told me of a most curious incident which occurred in the 1960-61 season. Hounds were running just north of Lyndhurst and the line went right through Emery Down churchyard. By the time Colonel East and Frank Peachey arrived on the scene the entire pack was marking over one of the graves — although there seemed to be no apparent reason for this. Upon investigation the grave turned out to be that of the late Jack Candy. Hounds were withdrawn with some difficulty from the spot and Colonel East frankly admits that he is entirely unable to explain the incident.

On another occasion he was talking to a puppy-walker at a meet and she asked, "Oh, by the way Colonel, whatever happened to *Daffodil*?". Colonel East simply couldn't remember, so seeking out Frank Peachey, he asked him what had become of the hound in question. Frank's reply was swift and to the point. "Shot the bugger!" he replied. The Master rode back to the lady and with great diplomacy told her the facts. "Oh that hound you were enquiring about . . . he was drafted to America".

Ralph Hill also came into the country from elsewhere. He had previously hunted with the **H.H.** and had moved to Burley at the end of World War II with his wife, Jane.

MRS SCOTT

These two Masters were joined in 1960 by Mrs Bridget Scott. She had previously been with the **Hursley**, an adjacent pack, and had seen that Hunt through an equally difficult period. Early in her first season there, during 1954, her Joint Master, Captain Faber, died suddenly, and although she was a stranger to that country she had courageously, and most successfully, carried on alone.

It was Mrs Scott who introduced Sir Richard Newton Rycroft as a potential new Joint Master when Geoffrey East and Ralph Hill expressed their intention to resign. She knew Sir Newton, as he is known, from beagling circles, and of course he was already well known as a noted hound breeder. His flair, backed by the courage of his convictions, had resulted in a beagle pack with a great reputation for work, quite apart from their enviable success on the flags.

SIR NEWTON RYCROFT

So it was that a new Mastership began in 1962 which consisted of Sir Newton, Mrs Scott and Brigadier Jefferies. The Brigadier was the 'local' sportsman of the trio, having been born and brought up at Cadnam, in the Forest, and had long hunted with the N.F.H. He had been Chairman of the Hunt for a short period from 1960-1962, (following Sir George Meyrick's resignation from that office, and subsequent death). In addition he was the only one of the trio to be actually resident in the country at that time. Sir Newton was still a Joint Master of the **Dummer Beagles** that first season, and was commuting back and forth to 'Little Rissington', his home in Gloucestershire.

As a matter of interest, Sir Newton had briefly carried the horn at the **Vine Hunt** on a number of occasions, during the winter of 1947, one of the severest winters on record. The next really severe winter was, co-incidently, 1962, when he first started hunting the New Forest Hounds. In parts of the south that year, 34 degrees of frost were recorded and although, as usual, the Forest escaped the worst of it, he recalls that all they seemed to do that first season was "plod around in the snow".

Sir Newton was born on 23rd January, 1918, and brought up at Dummer in North Hampshire. His father was Sir Nelson Rycroft, Master of the **Vine Hunt** from 1932-1938. This family had, in fact, produced five generations of Masters of the **Vine** and one — Mr Newton Fellowes — had founded the **Eggesford** in 1798, and was subsequently Master of the **Warwickshire**. Sir Newton represents the seventh generation of his family to be an M.F.H.!

He was educated at Winchester, and went on to Christ Church, Oxford where, a "brilliant scholar", he gained a B.A. in 1939. He had hunted with the **Vine**, as a child of course, but it was the pure science of venery that attracted him more than anything else. In 1939 he formed his own pack — **The Dummer Beagles**. At that time they hunted over the **Vine, Craven** and parts of the **H.H.** countries. Daphne Moore in her book *In Nimrod's Footsteps*, says of them, ". . . with their drive and cry they were a delight; in addition they were, in appearance, the most beautiful little Beagle pack that I have ever had the good fortune to behold".

Their Master served during the war as an S.O.E. officer on special work in the Balkans, having what has been described to me by a friend as "a tremendous war". He was mentioned in despatches and decorated by the King of Greece. Due to this war service the **Dummer Beagles** had had to be disbanded in 1943, although a few breeding bitches were kept. The pack next hunted again from Dummer in 1946, moving to 'Little Rissington' in the early 'fifties when Sir Newton, now married, moved there. The pack still hunt from 'Little Rissington' today.

On 11th August, 1962, cubhunting began, with Sir Newton hunting the New Forest Hounds from Rufus Stone. Poor Frank Peachey had tragically died of cancer the previous year and Peter Smith, formerly the whipper-in, had temporarily filled the sad breach until April '62. Sir Newton brought in Harry Lenthall as kennel-huntsman and he, like Jack Candy, was a genuine lover of hounds and simply lived for them!

PRIORITIES

In the previous season 1961-62 the tally had been only three brace. Clearly, the new Master's task was to teach the hounds to hunt and to draw and, vitally important in this heavily wooded country, to speak. All this he immediately set about doing, recruiting the assistance of an older experienced hound, from Sir Peter Farquar, which came via the **College Valley.** This hound had a particularly distinctive voice, and went a long way towards teaching the others what was required of them.

In the teeth of disapproval he began to experiment with French and Welsh outcrosses to improve both voice and scenting ability, sending New Forest bitches to carefully selected stallion hounds. *Trollop '64* and *Tension '65*, two good hounds, were from litters resulting from these visits, however the outstanding success from this policy was, of course, *Medyg '69*.

MEDYG

Medyg was from the first litter of Welsh outcross puppies by *Plas Macynleth Miller '63*, out of *New Forest Traffic '65*. From the first, *Medyg* proved to be remarkable, both in his working ability and, subsequently, as a sire of equally good progeny.

Sir Newton is on record as saying that, "after watching him hunt, I used to go home and sit down at my desk to look at *Medyg's* pedigree. From this I could see lots of reasons why he should be good, but no reasons why he should be outstanding. His litter sister *Marvel*, which went to Colonel Mitchell at the **Hambledon**, was equally brilliant". Therefore, he went back to *Plas Machynleth* to trace the history of *Medyg*'s antecedents, to find that his line goes back in direct tail male to the great *Gelligaer Topper*; arguably the best Welsh hound ever.

However, this is jumping forward in time and ignoring the problems of the early years of his Mastership. Brigadier Jeffries remained for two seasons and Mrs Scott for a further three seasons until 1967. Sir Newton feels that she was largely responsible for putting the Hunt back on its feet.

Figure 12.3 Sir Newton and his Hounds at a meet in the North of the Forest, 1970.

(*Photo courtesy*: Jim Mead)

FAMILY TRADITION

In 1962, when Brigadier Jeffries had become Joint Master, he had resigned the Chairmanship, because under the present rules no-one person can hold both offices. When this happened Mr Peter J. Green of 'Minstead Manor' became Chairman. Mr Green is the grandson of Mr Henry Francis Compton, (M.F.H. 1900-1905 and Chairman 1927-39), and was Mr Compton's heir. He continued the active and unstinting support that the Compton family have always given the Hunt. His wife, Mrs Susan Green who was daughter of the previous Master, Sir George Meyrick, was one of those dauntingly brilliant lady riders of the post-war years. She had often whipped-in to her father, and I am told that she had a wonderful way with hounds, for she merely had to "chirrup at them", in order to have them do exactly what she wanted of them.

Mr Green resigned the Chairmanship in 1970, and this important task was taken on by Mr Arthur Rickman of Brockenhurst, who still serves in this capacity. Although he can no longer ride to hounds for health reasons, Arthur never misses a day and is always to be seen, with a terrier or two at his heels and with a saucy remark flung after a disappearing rider.

BREEDING POLICY VINDICATED

From 1967 until 1971 Sir Newton was sole Master, and continued to hunt hounds himself. Sport had improved tremendously and hounds were achieving a growing reputation. The value of his outcross breeding policy became accepted, as the results were obvious. Although, to be accurate, most of the opposition had been centred around the French outcrosses rather that the Welsh, and these protests concerned mainly the technical difficulties surrounding entry in the F.K.S.B. (Foxhound Kennel Stud Book) of any progency from such a union; the French hound concerned being entered to deer and not fox.

In 1971 Sir Newton was advised by his doctors to give up hunting hounds himself, and those who know him will appreciate what a blow this must have been to him at the time. A Joint Master was, therefore, brought in: Major Peter Wainright, from the **Axe Vale** — a harrier pack that hunt the fox. Major Wainright brought with him George Watkins as kennel-huntsman, who "swopped" with Harry Lenthall, Harry going to the **Axe Vale**, where he is still.

Unfortunately, Major Wainright stayed for only one season before he moved on. I understand that he is now hunting a pack in Canada, where they have a very short season, being 'snowed up' from January onwards.

AMATEUR HUNTSMAN

At this jointure Sir Newton decided to cultivate some 'home-grown' talent and asked Mr Frank Pearson to come in as an amateur huntsman. Frank had no previous experience with hounds whatsoever, other than as a mounted follower, and recent puppy walker. In fact, until recently, his main interest had been gun dogs! He told me that he thought he only got the job by default, "Everyone else had turned it down", but I doubt if Sir Newton would agree with this interpretation. Anyway he accepted with alacrity, and after being nudged in gently — Sir Newton initially sharing the hunting week — he eventually took over altogether just in time for the opening meet.

To use Frank's own words, "Undoubtedly the greatest problem that I had overcome, was myself, and especially my inexperience. My greatest aids were Sir Newton (every post brought a letter from him on a topic relating to hounds, it was all most exciting), he was very patient; and *Medyg* and his family who helped me on every occasion".

From 1974 Mr Jeremy Whaley, also an amateur, turned hounds to him, George Watkins continuing as kennel-huntsman, and this combination went on until 1977 when Frank left to become Master of the **Brecon**. He is presently Master of the **South Herefordshire**.

THIRD GENERATION

Upon Frank's resignation, Sir Newton brought in Richard Perry as huntsman, with Mr Whaley remaining as amateur whipper-in, George Watkins also left at this time to go to the **Banwen Miners Hunt**, where he remained until April, 1980.

Richard was the son of Ralph, and the grandson of Fred Perry, both of whom it will be recalled had previously hunted these hounds. Indeed Richard was actually born at the huntsman's cottage at 'Minstead', so he could hardly be termed a newcomer to the country. After two seasons, however, he left the Forest to go as huntsman to the **Albrighton**, in 1979.

THE CURRENT SCENE

Mr Jeremy Whaley, amateur whipper-in since 1974, then took over as amateur huntsman. He had the advantages of not only knowing the country well but of already having forged a good working relationship with the hounds. Albert Harris, as kennel-huntsman now occupies the huntsman's cottage at the kennels and his capable wife, Joan, is a second mother to sick hounds and whelps. Albert was twenty-one seasons with the **South Devon**, before coming to the Forest.

Here is a hunt servant of the 'old school', from the same mould as Jack Candy. Hounds and their welfare being not merely a job to him but a life-long love. Due to his patient, loving and skilled hard work hounds have never been seen in such fine fettle or happier spirit.

Other changes concern the Honorary Secretaryship. Mrs Pat DuPré resigned this post in 1972 after sixteen years of indefatigable service to the Hunt. Mrs Jane Boyce then took over for one season, since when this important role has been filled by Mrs Jane Hill — wife of ex-M.F.H., Ralph Hill.

The remarkable *Medyg* is now in his tenth season. He has descendants in forty kennels in the United Kingdom, and four generations of his progeny are hunting in the Forest at this time. His son *Badminton Monmouth '78* was the Champion Doghound at Peterborough in 1978, and his offspring continue to carry off all major awards in the foxhound show world.

So the New Forest Hounds approach the Hunt's 200th anniversary and it seems that it is in a very strong position to weather another 200 years.

Indeed the season 1979-80 was said by many to be a return to a "Golden Age" of New Forest hunting. Mr Whaley has shown extra-ordinarily fine sport. He is patient and watchful and helps his hounds only when they require assistance. Consequently, when they go away on a line you'd better be close in-touch, or else all will be over with you for that day, for they go like blazes and in the thickly wooded enclosure are soon lost to the lagards.

Mr Jim Loader turns hounds to him, assisted occasionally by Mr Steve Ward and Mr Giles Verdon. Jim is one of the best mounted men in the Forest, breeding all of his delightful, clever little horses and subsequently making them. It is a treat to watch him quietly, efficiently and methodically going about his duties in the field.

It has one of the best ever packs of working hounds, and as keen a following of members and supporters as one could wish for. In addition it has the experience and valued service of the Chairman (eleven years), the Master (eighteen years), and the Honorary Secretary (seven years).

Hounds can no longer hunt through April into May, so that the lovely tradition of spring hunting in the Forest has lapsed. This is mainly due to the recent massive influx of tourists; those that flock here each summer to see the Forest for its sheer beauty. However, in the winter months we have its loveliness to ourselves, and we count ourselves enormously privileged to hunt over it. Sir Newton usually manages one or two early April days though.

Certainly the country is changed, for many reasons, and the old stagers will tell you that it can never be what it was. But it is **less** changed than most other hunting countries. The Hunt still has enormous freedom over 90 square miles of woodland and heathland. There is no scarcity of foxes, in fact quite the reverse. Only two seasons ago I witnessed a leash put up by hounds in Appleslade Enclosure, hounds set off on the line of one, a second ran heel through the pack whilst the third was, for a time, actually running with hounds until he sensibly and quietly dropped back. In the event all three escaped with their brushes intact as the hunted one went to ground in a badger earth!

In spite of the fact that the Forest no longer draws the crowds for spring hunting we still attract small numbers of visitors wishing to extend their season by joining us for early cubhunting in August and September, or late hunting in early April. What can be more delightful than our small merry fields of a dozen or so setting off at the crack of a misty, cobwebby autumn dawn?

A word of warning to anyone reading these pages and intending to visit the Forest. The bogs are not nearly so intimidating as one is led to believe and if you pick a green collar as a pilot you will probably survive. But never, never, follow the Master through a bog. Many have tried it— Sir Newton always gets across, and we have never been able to explain how or why **anyone** who tries to follow ends up wallowing!

The Supporters' Club, set up by Ralph Hill in 1957, still flourishes and is of tremendous assistance under the present Chairmanship of Mr E. Gailor, in supporting the upkeep of the hounds. Among our most valued supporters are Mr George Crouch and Mr Harry Blandford — earth stoppers *extraordinaire*. Both are over seventy but neither misses a day, being first to arrive at the meets and last to leave in the evening. Mr Gerald Hill never misses either, and pops up from the deepest scrub, frequently ahead of the mounted field with the inevitable terrier and a friendly word.

RIDING MEMBERS

Of current Hunt Club members, those who presently ride regularly to hounds are as follows: Sir Newton Rycroft, Bart., M.F.H., Mr M. Bedwell; Mr J. Belcher; Mr P. Cross; Mr B. Dowsett; Mr R. Hill; Mr K. Hobbs; Mr J. Hopkinson; Mr R. Jenkins; Mr G. Painter; Dr A. Page; Mr G. Scholes; Mr D. Smith; and Mr L. Trafford.

Whilst the ladies are represented by Lady Ann Rycroft; Mrs D. Barker; Mrs J. Boyce; Mrs P. Cross; Miss C. Davenport; Mrs J. East; Mrs R. Hill; Miss P. Hudson; Miss P. Mayer; Mrs M. Paice; Miss P. Pannell; Mrs L. Trafford, Miss M. Trafford and myself.

FAMILY NAMES

These are only a few representative names of those who follow both mounted and afoot, and actively support the New Forest Hounds today. A complete list would take an entire chapter, but it is interesting to note that among the current Hunt Club membership lists there are still some of those old familiar names that have continuously cropped up throughout the history of the Hunt: Pulteney; Meyrick; Morant and of course the Compton family, now represented by Mr Peter Green.

Hunter Trials

The latest major venture of The Supporters' Club is a new hunter trial course. A stiff, permanent course, professionally laid out on land kindly loaned by Mr C. Pilkington. Administered by a hard working committee headed by Mr Tony Taylor, it has been planned to attract top class, cross-country riders to the twice annual events to be held in the spring and autumn.

'EPILOGUE'

There can be no real end to this history because it is still being made. As long as there is foxhunting, there will be a pack in the New Forest and I can think of no better way to end this book than to quote the final part of the late George Eyre Matcham's poem:

> **"The first wish of my heart till I have to depart,**
> **And extinguished are life's dying embers,**
> **Is 'Luck and Good Sport of the very best sort**
> **To the New Forest Hounds, and its members."**

HUNTING DIARY 1962-1980

April 1963

"On 4th April the Duke of Beaufort brought his bitch pack by invitation for a day's hunting in the New Forest. The meet was at Janesmoor Pond where a large field with many visitors from neighbouring packs was assembled. The many distinguished looking strangers and beautiful horses provided a splendid sight, which many old timers said reminded them of the old days when Spring Hunting in the New Forest was very fashionable, and people brought their strings of hunters down to finish the season.

"The first draw, North Bentley Wood, proved blank, as did Holly Hatch and Broomy, but by the banks of Dockens Water below Broomy hounds got away to a good start on a big dog fox. They went away at a great pace, and with a wonderful cry, into Holly Hatch and then up the hill through Broomy fields and down the enclosure leaving by the bottom corner, hounds raced away to High Corner, thence across to Milkam and through Roe Wood still going a great pace. They then pushed their fox out through Pinnick Wood and Little Linford out to Picket Box. By Shobley they checked momentarily then picked up the line again and hunted up the box to the big earth near the main road. The fox found this stopped so went on over the main Ringwood Road across Hightown Common through Windwhistle, coming out onto the open Forest again. Scent was evidently failing on a beaten fox, and he was given up just short of Knaves Ash. This was a 6 mile point and it was indeed a pity that hounds did not get their reward. Still it was an education and a delight to see this brilliant pack work, and we hope all our visitors enjoyed it as much as we did."

Taken from *Horse and Hound Magazine*, written by Pat DuPré.

(Note: It is interesting to note that during Sir Newton's Mastership the following packs, in addition to the Duke of Beaufort's have visited by invitation: the Milvain (twice); Cattistock; South Dorset (twice); South & West Wiltshire; Mr Goschen's; Cotswold Farmers; Tiverton; Hambledon; Eridge; the Berkeley; Bicester & Warden Hill and the Tedworth.)

10th December, 1963

"Royal Oak, Bank. Plenty of foxes in Hurst Hill but very little scent. Marked a vixen to ground near the Buckhound kennels and bolted a dog fox from the same earth. He ran over the Brockenhurst Road, sharp left recrossed the road and to ground again. Bolted again and achieved a nice hunt of 60 minutes: Over the grass to New Park right handed, over the Brockenhurst Road, all around Ramnor, Pignall and top of Hurst Hill lost on a carpet of dead leaves in Park grounds."

14th December, 1965

"Ocknell Pond. Found A & O Plot opposite Eyeworth Lake, ran Eyeworth Wood, all round Island Thorns and lost after 20 minutes very fast. Found Rifle Butts Gorse, fox taking bad line to Godshill. Found Pitts Wood and had glorious 90 minutes, nearly all over the open Moorland of the Ashley Hills, eventually losing him when he came back to main road in failing light."

24th Feburary, 1970

"Bushey Bratley. Ran hard but inconclusively around Roe and Milkham for 2 hours. Then had a brilliant hunt from Little Linford. Ran up the Heath to a big and well stopped earth at the top of Shobley Bottom, over the main A31, through Foulford Bottom, over Burley Street Road, left Ridley Wood on the right, ran past Burley Old House, right through Soldiers Bog, left through Bratley Wood over Boldrewood Green road, recrossed A31 at Ocknell underpass, fast to New Slufters and caught their fox at the North end. A very fast 45 minutes, hounds quite untouched and a point of 5½ miles — perhaps 9 miles as they ran."

13th February, 1971

"Brockenhurst Bridge. Dog fox from New Park straight to ground. Bolted and had enjoyable 45 minutes all around Warwick Slade, Queens Bower, Brick Kilns and to ground in New Park. Evicted. Found Poundhill and lost on Ornamental Drive. Found American Strawberries, some local hunting around Clumbers and Aldridge Hill before he ran by Pound Hill, Queens Bower, Brick Kiln and Hurst Hill to the main Brockenhurst Road at Clayhill. Cry obliterated by roar of traffic, slipped over unattended right through Brockenhurst Woodlands, over main electric line (most probably by Bridge) and killed in New Copse. A great hunt in 40 minutes, untouched and a 4½ mile point."

All the above extracts were written by Sir Newton Rycroft.

18th December, 1973

"Killed the 1,000th fox of Sir Newton's Mastership, in Millersford Bottom, having found in Turf Hill Enclosure."

Boxing Day, 1973

"A really good day, though no great point was made hounds hunted hard all day and accounted for 1½ brace."

Tuesday, 1st January, 1974

"Met at Ocknell Pond, 18 couples out. Some local hunting in the morning. Then, found at Milkham and ran at best pace to Red Shoot Wood, High Corner Wood, running the stone road to Broomy Enclosure, away as if for Hasley then left handed along Linwood Bog, over to the Spinney at Linwood, on to Roe Cottage, slowly up to Buckherd Bottom, fresh found and back to Roe Cottage, Red Shoot Wood, Appleslade, great Linford, over Rockford Common and to ground in Beacon Hill Coppice. A 3½ mile point and 13 miles as hounds ran in 2hrs 20mins."

Saturday, 16th February

"Met at Brockenhurst Bridge, with 14½ couple. After some local hunting in the morning, accounting for a fox, we found in Woodfidley and he went to ground at once. He was soon bolted and ran out to Stubby Copse, over to Pignall and ran the stone roads all the way to Park Hill, then down to Denny Wood, crossed the Beaulieu Road for Matley Wood, then right handed through the bogs to cross the Southampton road near Ashurst Lodge. Through Ironshill and Busketts into the fields behind Busketts Lawn Hotel and into Fletchwood Enclosure and stopped hounds in the dark. 1hr 25mins, 5 mile point — 10 as hounds ran, and only four horses up at the end."

(Author's Note: Oddly, we had several similar runs in subsequent years.)

Saturday, 2nd March

"Met at Rufus Stone with 16½ couple. Killed a poor fox in Slufters, then found again in New Slufters. Hounds settled well and ran as if to cross the main road below Bushey Bratley. Turning left from here he left cover and crossed Bratley Plain and into Roe Wood near Roe East Gate, through here to Roe Cottage and out into Red Shoot Wood, Webbs Copse, Great Linford over Rockford Common and killed at Waterslade Farm. A first Class hunt at best pace all the way with only one check. A 4 mile point— 7 miles as hounds ran and all in 40 minutes."

1976

"This was a super season with a new record tally of 59½ brace. Many good hunts were scored. Probably my best hunt in the Forest occurred on Tuesday, 10th February, 1976.

"We met at Godshill Gravel Pit, the morning producing some moderate hunting around Godshill and Island Thorns. The last draw was at 3.30 at Amberwood and we found in a small clump of rhododendrons. Hounds were on good terms and scent was improving. He ran on into Alder Hill, out and up onto Hampton Ridge and into Island Thorns, which was the last time I saw any of the Field. Galloping hard now it was extremely difficult to keep in touch with hounds as they left Island Thorns for Studly Castle and crossed the Southampton Road just below Bramshaw Telegraph. Racing on through Franchise Wood they crossed into Lyburn, and out onto Hampworth Common before swinging back behind No Man's Land over Pipers Wait and through Bramshaw Wood. I got up to them in the dark on Furzley Common at Plaitford. The whole hunt was without a check, the longest point 6½ miles and it was at least 14 miles as hounds ran."

All the above extracts are from the hunting diaries of Frank Pearson.

Tuesday, February 5th, 1980

"Hounds scored a marvellous hunt today, having found in the far end of Buskett's Lawn. They were off like smoke, slipping most of the large mounted field, through Buskett's, into Rushpole Wood, across Foxhill Common and crossed the Cadnam Road into Pikes Hill. Ran into Northerwood and over to Lyndhurst Hill, closely, not to say jealously, followed by all that remained of the field (besides Jeremy)—John Belcher, Lady Rycroft, George Painter and myself. I think he may have been slightly headed here but ran on through White Moor, White Shoot, Knightwood Oak, crossed the Ornamental, swung left, and ran and crossed the A35 through heavy but well behaved traffic. Into Brock Hill and to ground at the top of a rise. A point of 5 miles in 45 minutes. Jeremy and the smug quartet in touch the entire hunt and none of them prepared to give an inch during what I consider to be the best run so far this season."

From the author's hunting diary.

Figure 12.4 Medyg

A most famous foxhound. Autumn, 1976.

(*Photo courtesy*: Jim Mead)

NEW FOREST HUNT POEMS 3

In December, 1978, Mr Dorian Williams was to autograph copies of his recently published book *Master of One* at Beales in Bournemouth. As a publicity "stunt" the N.F.H. were asked to provide a hound for photographs and the resulting incident involving the Forest's best loved and highly celebrated hound sparked off the following ditty:

MEDYG GOES TO TOWN

A famous Foxhunter to Bournemouth would go
To autograph books was his mission,
So the publishers hit on a capital scheme
And provided a hound in addition.

For the book was on hunting and horses and things,
(And if we buy one who can blame us?)
So the hound they requested was gallant and bold,
And certainly quite the most famous.

Down in the Forest old *Medyg* **was puzzled**
When Master and Richard pursued him,
And he wondered just what the devil was up
When they polished and combed and shampoo'd him.

So all bright and shiny and smelling quite sweet,
Our star travelled up in some state.
To a big flashy Store in the best part of town,
Where the cameras and press stood in wait.

"It's *Medyg*, **Hooray!" the crowds all proclaim,**
The Commissionaire sprang to attention
Medyg **just sniffed and lifted his leg,**
And what he did next I can't mention.

He greeted the author with nonchalant air
And posed for the cameras with grace
But all he could think of with nose all aquiver,
Was the terrible smell in the place.

For the store in their wisdom had chosen,
The most suitable section for sure!
The Perfumery Section was perfect,
Just inside the main doors on ground floor.

It happened just as he was leaving
A most terrible thing, as you'll learn
A spray of perfume, misdirected,
Covered *Medyg* **from nose back to stern.**

Now when he arrived back in kennels
The others went red in the face
And *Paragon* **said, very clearly,**
He thought it a Public Disgrace!

But the ladies were totally different,
And into his arms they would dive,
For as *Valour* **related to** *Maxime*,
"I'm sure it's Chanel Number Five"!

So when in the Forest and *Medyg* floats by,
Don't whistle and smile and shout "Cutie".
For when all's said and done, and remember this please,
He *was* only doing his duty!

M.S. Lovell

Bibliography

Acton, C.R., *Sport & Sportsmen in The New Forest*, 1936
Apperley, C.J. "Nimrod", *Hunting Reminiscences*, 1826
Beckford, Peter, *Thoughts upon Hunting*, 1796
Berkeley, Grantley, *Reminiscences of a Huntsmen*, 1897
Berry, Michael, *Foxhunting from The Times*, 1933
Bradley, *Foxhunting From Shire to Shire*, 1912
Buchanan-Jardine, Sir John, *Hounds of the World*, 1937
Carr, Raymond, *English Foxhunting*, 1976
"Cecil", *Records of The Chase*, 1854
Clarke, John, *Life & Times of George III*, 1972
Clayton, Michael, *A Hunting We Will Go*, 1967
Cobbett, William, *Rural Rides*, 1853
Cook, Colonel John, *Observations on Hunting*, 1826
Cuming, E.D., *Squire Osbaldeston, his Biography*, 1926
"The Druid", *Post & Paddock*, 1857
"The Druid", *Silk & Scarlet*, 1859
"The Druid", *Scott & Sebright*, 1854
Edwards, Lionel, *Reminiscences of a Sporting Artist*, 1947
Fitt, H.N., *Covertside Sketches*, 1878
Graham, Sir Reginald, *Foxhunting Recollections*, 1908
Heysham, W.N. ("Aesop"), *Sporting Reminiscences of Hampshire*, 1864
Higginson, A. Henry, *The Meynell of The West*, 1936
Hutchinson, Horace, *The New Forest*, 1906
Hugh, Macartsland, *Old Sporting*, 1948
Hope, Big. J.F.R., *A History of Hunting in Hampshire*, 1950
Joseph, Michael, *The English Squire and His Sport*, 1977
Lascelles, Hon. Gerald, *Thirty-five Years in The New Forest*, 1915
Moore, Daphne, *Famous Foxhunters*, 1978
Moore, Daphne, *In Nimrod's Footsteps*, 1974
Paget, Otho, *Hunting*, 1900
Sexaguarian, *Reminiscences of the Vyne Hounds*, 1854
Stevens, F., *New Forest Beautiful*, 1925
Stirling, A.M., *Diaries of Dummer*, re-published 1934
Warner, Richard, *Literary Recollections*, 1830
Warner, Richard, *Companion on tour of Lymington*, 1780
Watson, J.N.P., *The Book of Foxhunting*, 1977
Wilmot, Sir John Eardley, *Reminiscences of Thomas Asheton-Smith*, 1862
York, Edward, 2nd Duke of, *The Master of Game*, republished 1904

Various issues of the following periodicals:

Baily's Magazine, 1870-1926
Baily's Hunting Directory, 1906-1979
Horse & Hound, 1884-1979
Annals of Sport, 1815-1830
The Sporting Magazine, 1780-1832
British Sports and Sportsmen, Past Vols. 1 and 2, c. 1904
Hampshire and some neighbouring records, c. 1900

NEW FOREST HUNT CLUB

Date	*Chairman*	*Hon. Sec.*	*Master of Foxhounds*	
1781			Mr Vincent H. Gilbert	
1798		Mr S. Williams	Committee	
1800		Mr S. Williams	Mr John Compton	
1803	A.B. Drummond	Mr S. Williams	Committee	
1808	Lord Cavan	Unknown	John Warde	
1814	Lord Cavan	Unknown	S. Nicolls	
1828	Unknown	Unknown	W. Wyndham	
1838	H.C. Compton	Col. G. Robbins	C. Codrington	
1842	W. Sloane-Stanley	Col. G. Robbins	L. Sheddon	
1849	W. Sloane-Stanley	Mr Walter Williams	L. Sheddon	
1853	A. Drummond	Martin Powell	Mr Theobald	
1854	A. Drummond	Martin Powell	Rev. E. Timson	
1860	A. Drummond	Martin Powell	Captain Morant	
1866	Sir H. Paulett	Martin Powell	Captain Morant	
1869	Sir H. Paulett	Martin Powell	William Standish	
1874	Sir H. Paulett	Martin Powell	Sir Reginald Graham	
1878	Sir H. Paulett	Martin Powell	Mr George Meyrick	
			Country Divided	
			Eastern	**Western**
1885	Sir H. Paulett	Martin Powell	Major Browne	J. Mills
1886	Lord Montague	Martin Powell	F. Bradburne	J. Mills
1887	Lord Montague	Ernest Wingrove	F. Bradburne	J. Mills
1889	Lord Montague	Ernest Wingrove	S. Pearce	J. Mills
1891	Lord Montague	Ernest Wingrove	S. Pearce	Sir G. Thursby
1894	Lord Montague	Ernest Wingrove	H.M. Powell	Sir G. Thursby
			Country Reunited	
1895	Lord Montague	Ernest Wingrove	H. Martin Powell	
1899	Lord Montague	Ernest Wingrove	C. Heseltine	
1900	Lord Montague	Ernest Wingrave	Henry F. Compton	
1905	Sir G. Meyrick	Ernest Wingrove	H. Martin Powell	
1907	Sir G. Meyrick	Ernest Wingrove	W.D.P. Cazenove	
1912	Sir G. Mayrick	Ernest Wingrove	Mr. Cooke-Hurle & Lt. Col. Cooke-Hurle	

Date	*Chairman*	*Hon. Sec.*	*Master of Foxhounds*
1913	Sir G. Meyrick	Ernest Wingrove	Lt. Col. Cooke-Hurle
1914	Sir G. Meyrick	Ernest Wingrove	Lt. Col. Cooke-Hurle & Major Timson
1915	Sir G. Meyrick	Ernest Wingrove	Major T. Timson
1916	Sir G. Meyrick	Ernest Wingrove	Committee
1919	Sir G. Meyrick	Ernest Wingrove	Major G. Meyrick
1927	H.F. Compton	Ernest Wingrove	Major G. Meyrick (now Sir G. Meyrick)
1932	H.F. Compton	George Ferguson	Sir G. Meyrick
1939	H.F. Compton	P.P. Curtis	Sir G. Meyrick
1943	Sir George Meyrick	P.P. Curtis	Sir G. Meyrick
1950	Sir George Meyrick	P.P. Curtis & J.N. Faire	Sir G. Meyrick
1956	Sir George Meyrick	L.P. DuPré	Committee
1958	Sir George Meyrick	L.P. DuPré	Darling/East/Hill
1960	Brig. Jeffries	L.P. DuPré	East/Hill/Scott
1962	P. Green	L.P. DuPré	Scott/Jeffries/Sir R.N. Rycroft
1964	P. Green	L.P. DuPré	Scott/Sir R.N. Rycroft
1967	P. Green	L.P. DuPré	Sir R.N. Rycroft
1970	A. Rickman	L.P. DuPré	Sir R.N. Rycroft
1972	A. Rickman	L.P. DuPré	Sir R.N Rycroft & P. Wainright
1973	A. Rickman	Jane Boyce	Sir R.N. Rycroft
1974	A. Rickman	Jane Hill	Sir R.N. Rycroft

Members of Committees

1798-1800 Mr Drummond, Sir P. Jennings-Clarke, Mr John Compton
1803-1808 Lord Cavan, Mr Charles Mitchell, Mr S. Williams
1916-1919 Major T. Timson, Captain Compton, Mr M. Powell, Mr Thursby, Mr Downman
1956-1958 Sir George Meyrick, Ralph Hill, John Morant, Mr & Mrs J.N. Faire, Mr L.C. Martin, Major & Mrs Dunlop, Mrs Rayner, Sir Gervaise Tennyson, Sq. Ldr. Vernon Simmons.

INDEX

Q

R

S

T

V

Y